Fruit of the Spirit

The Keys to a Christian Personality

Ron Hembree

SPIRE

Copyright © 1969 by Baker Books
Published by Fleming H. Revell
a division of Baker Book House Company
P.O. Box 6287, Grand Rapids, MI 49516-6287

ISBN: 0-8007-8615-7

Fourth printing, June 1996

Printed in the United States of America

Formerly published as *Pocket of Pebbles: Inspirational
Thoughts on the Fruits of the Spirit* and *Fruits of the
Spirit*

Fruit
of the
Spirit

To Dad, a Father and a Friend

Contents

Preface

An ancient fable tells of three merchants crossing the Arabian Desert. Traveling in darkness to avoid the intense heat one starless night, they were passing over a dry creek bed when a voice from the blackness commanded them to halt. They were then ordered to stoop, pick up pebbles from the creek bed, and put them in their pockets.

After obeying the strange command, they were told to leave that place, camping nowhere near. The mysterious voice then told them that in the morning they would be both happy and sad. Shaken and confused, and obeying the mysterious intruder, they traveled through the night.

When morning came, the men anxiously looked into their pockets, and rather than finding the pebbles as expected, there were precious jewels. They, indeed, were happy and sad. They were happy they had picked up the jewels, but sad because while they had the opportunity they had not picked up many more.

This legend beautifully expresses how many feel about the unsearchable riches of God's Word. We are thrilled we have absorbed as much as we have, but sad because we have not absorbed much more. Specifically, I feel this way about two dynamic verses in Galatians, "But the fruit of the Spirit is love, joy, peace, longsuffering, gentleness, goodness, faith, meekness, temperance: against such there is no law" (5:22, 23).

For many years I have read these words, pondered them, and even preached about them. Then one day, in the dawn of God's illuminating Spirit, I again looked carefully and prayerfully and found these not ordinary words, but fantastic portraits of truth. Rather than just pebbles stuffed into my spiritual intellect, I found them priceless jewels. My heart soared in keen joy with this illumination, but saddened that I had not before so deeply appreciated their value.

Much has been said about what constitutes a Christian. Some can tell us the many ingredients which go into the making of a Christian personality. Most people can tell us what a Christian is not. However, never have I read so clearly the exact definition of the total Christian personality than in these two Galatian verses. It is as though all principles of the New Testament are wrapped up here. Christ cogently condensed Christian *responsibility* into two commandments—Love God with all your heart and your neighbor as yourself. Similarly, Paul succinctly sets down the Christian *personality* in these Galatian verses.

I pray that these words we have so long heard and sometimes pondered will suddenly come alive as God's Holy Spirit illuminates them to our spirits. Jewels are only seen when light dances on them; so these priceless truths can only be understood as God's Holy Spirit leads us into their depth. The purpose of this book is to encourage believers to take these priceless jewels from their spiritual pockets and look again at them in the light of His Holy Spirit.

RON HEMBREE

1

Misled by a Miracle

A little of hell spilled over on the world because two people believed in a false prophet. In his brilliant book, *Nicholas and Alexandra*, Robert K. Massie tells how the Tsar and Empress of Russia were misled by a miracle and thus brought their great empire down to dust.

After many years of anxious waiting for an heir to the Russian throne, Tsar Nicholas II and his German wife, Federovna, were blessed with a son. However, their hopes for the future were cruelly crushed six weeks later when doctors discovered the infant had hemophilia, an incurable blood disease that could kill at any moment. All of his short life was to be lived in the shadow of terror, with death stalking every footstep. This tragedy introduced into the royal family one of the most evil men who ever lived.

Several times the young tsarevich slipped close to death. Seeing him writhe in excruciating pain, his tormented parents would beg doctors to do something, but they were helpless. In those moments they turned to Gregory Rasputin, a religious mystic of questionable credentials, later known as the mad monk of Russia. Invariably, he would pray for the boy and there would be a marked improvement. Even today doctors are at a loss to explain how these healings took place, but history testifies to them. Always, Rasputin would warn the parents the boy would only live as long as they listened to him.

Rasputin's power over the royal family became so great he could, with a word, obtain the appointment or dismissal of any government official. He had men appointed or dismissed on the basis of their attitudes toward himself rather than their abilities. Consequently, the whole Russian government reeled under the unwise counsel of this evil man. Seeds of revolution were planted and watered with discontent. It erupted into the murder of the royal family, internal war, and the communistic takeover. Alexander Kerensky, a key government figure during those trying times, later reflected, "Without Rasputin, there could have been no Lenin."

Men have always been impressed with miracles and miracle workers. In the case of the Russian rulers, one can readily understand their heartbreaking position and forgive them for their tragic mistake. However, in the cold light of history, one can also see the great tragedy dealt to the world because these two looked on the outward appearance.

Too often, men learn too little from the mistakes of others. Today, some are still being lead astray by the spectacular. Jesus echoes the sentiment of this age when he says, "An evil and adulterous generation seeketh after a sign . . ." (Matt. 12:39). Jesus taught us there is something more meaningful than miracles and more superb than the spectacular. He came not just to die, but to show us how to live and live in the proper perspective.

Winding up His Sermon on the Mount, Christ digresses a moment to warn of false prophets who would come in sheep's clothing. He then gives us the perfect formula for discerning who is of God and who is of Satan, "Wherefore, by their fruits ye shall know them" (Matt. 7:20). It is interesting to note He did not say, "Look for great signs, wonders, miracles, or the spectacular."

Rather, He simply said men are to be judged by what they *are,* not what they *do.*

This does not diminish the miracles of God or the gifts of the Spirit. God uses these in His own sovereign will to bring about His ultimate purpose. Paul lists these gifts as the word of wisdom, knowledge, healing, working of miracles, prophecy, discerning of spirits, divers kinds of tongues, and interpretation of tongues (1 Cor. 12:8-10). However, never does the Bible say we are to gauge a man's spirituality or sincerity by these gifts.

Miracles can be mimicked and gifts can be imitated. History is filled with cases where this is true. The miracles of Moses were copied to a degree by the magicians of Pharaoh. Pseudo-religious seers have healed for ages, and speaking in tongues has been copied time after time in pagan worship. If Christianity relied on these for its cornerstone, it would be merely another religion in a world choking with religion. But, Christ struck down this false appraisal forever when He declared, "By their fruits ye shall know them."

The fruit of the Spirit can never be imitated. It is what a person *is,* not what he *does.* This fruit crowds out all ambition. Gifts are external, but fruit is internal. Miracles fade, but fruit remains. The fruit of the spirit strikes through personal pride in anything we accomplish or in anything God does through us. No earthly man could or would want to imitate the true fruit of the Spirit.

These truths should not be foreign to us, since Christ taught them from the first moments of His life on this earth. We are staggered by the shocking simplicity with which Christ came and preached. Obscurity, poverty, and insignificance were the soil from which He sprang. God did not choose a castle, a king, a teeming city, or large headlines to announce His Son's coming, but slipped Him into the world unnoticed except by a few shepherds and mild mystics.

Even the Kingdom that Christ preached was likened to salt, seed, leaven, and light. His similies were indeed true

13

because the gospel permeated, germinated, expanded, and illumined until all other thoughts of men were pushed aside to make way for His Kingdom. The face of all history has been changed by this subtle but supernatural coming of the King of Kings and Lord of Lords.

Indeed, Christ did work many miracles and did great works. However, He chided some for following Him only because of His miracles and told others frankly, "See that thou tell no man." John intimated there were many great works and signs he performed that were not even recorded. Christ was not interested in stunning men with His power, but saving men by His blood. The ones Christ raised from the dead are now dead again. Those He healed have long been forgotten in flesh and remembered only in word. Those miracles and their immediate usefulness are now wasted, except for encouragement to remember Christ is the same yesterday, today, and forever. However, the Kingdom He preached has filled the whole earth with its influence just as He said it would.

The blackest hours in church history have been when men have emphasized the spectacular to the neglect of the fruit of the Spirit. Wars were waged in the name of the cross. Men were murdered because they did not comply. A militant black leader, the late Malcolm X, blamed Christianity for deep-seated hatred between the races and calls Christianity a white man's religion. Strangely, he admires Christ, but feels Christianity failed in following Jesus, emphasizing the external, neglecting the real truth of the Master. Perhaps he is right. Maybe we have so long tried to appear righteous on the outside that we have forgotten Christ is Lord of the heart, not the theater.

In this time of history it is of utmost importance we get back to the truths Christ taught and lived. Attacks have been and will be made against the church. Indignant leaders are turning an accusing finger at Christianity and claiming its irrelevance. Jesus said this time would come. But, in this time it is vital we have our proper perspective.

A Hebrew language scholar, John Marco Allegro, warns, "The church is going to be scourged as never before because . . . Christianity's roots lay in a drug-taking cult and the New Testament is just a cover story for it." He went on to say the Old Testament prophets were 'taking a trip' with a drug when they had their visions. The charge goes on: "Here is your speaking with tongues. Its priests and prophets were dope pushers. The New Testament was a cover document meant to circulate among the strange groups at that time who were under attack from the Roman establishment."

Those who know Christ and God's Word will not be shattered by such attacks. The truth is, the main of the message of the New Testament has little to do with miracles or signs. The crux of Christ's message and the apostles' admonition concerned the inner man and his development. The power of Christ is not in His miracles, but in His message.

We are now living in the day of false prophets. Today "a man's enemies are of his own household." The church is being attacked by its own unbelieving leaders who have the sheep's clothing of intellectual pursuit. These are trying times when we must know where we stand. We know not by miracles, but by fruit. The gates of hell shall not prevail, but it is time we buttressed ourselves for attack and stood firm in our conviction that God desires truth in the inward parts. It is important to remember, "For there shall arise false Christs, and false prophets, and shall show great signs and wonders; insomuch that, if it were possible, they shall deceive the very elect" (Matt. 24:24). Then, for our own lives, Peter's admonition to the ladies of the faith should be the guiding principle: "Whose adorning let it not be that outward adorning . . . But let it be the hidden man of the heart, in that which is not corruptible, even the ornament of a meek and quiet spirit, which is in the sight of God of great price" (1 Peter 3:3, 4).

15

The fruit of the Spirit is . . .   **love**

2

A Tree of Ribbons

Warden Kenyon J. Scudder tells of a friend riding on a train next to an obviously troubled and anxious young man. Finally, the boy blurted out that he was a convict returning from prison. His crime had brought shame on his poor but proud family and they had never visited or written him during the years he was away. He had hoped this was only that they were too poor to travel the long distance and too uneducated to write. However, he could not be sure they had forgiven.

The youth went on to explain he had wanted to make it easy for them. Therefore, he had written them, asking them to put up a signal when the train passed their little farm on the outskirts of the town. If they had forgiven and wanted him to return home they were to tie a white ribbon in the big apple tree near the tracks. If they did not want him back they were to do nothing and he would stay on the train, go west, and lose himself forever.

Nearing his home town, the youth's suspense and discomfort grew to the point where he could not look. His friend offered to watch for him and they changed places. A few minutes later he put his hand on the young convict's shoulder, whispered in a broken voice, "It's all right. *The whole tree is white with ribbons.*"

Later, this friend told Warden Scudder, "I felt as though I had witnessed a miracle." He had indeed. There is always something miraculous about deep and abiding love that transcends troubles and overrides natural tendencies of pride and hurt. It must have been such a moment when the song writer sensed the deepest love mortals have known when he penned:

> Marvelous grace of our loving Lord,
> Grace that exceeds our sin and our guilt,
> Yonder on Calvary's mount outpoured,
> There where the blood of the Lamb was spilt.

Then the poet echoes the beautiful refrain that still stirs the most seared of souls:

> Grace, grace, God's grace,
> Grace that will pardon and cleanse within;
> Grace, grace, God's grace,
> Grace that is greater than all our sin.

Redeemed man ponders the unmerited favor, forgiveness, and mercy of a loving God who has saved us in spite of weakness and wickedness. An aged minister lay dying when his faithful deacon said, "Ah, pastor, you are about to receive your reward." "Oh, no," replied the preacher with labored breath, "Not reward! Mercy!" David knew this boundless grace when he cried, "Have mercy upon me O God, *according to thy lovingkindness: according unto the multitude of thy tender mercies blot out my transgressions*" (Ps. 51:1). God has His whole tree spangled with white ribbons indicating His deep desire to forgive and reinstate fallen and wayward man.

Love so amazing, so divine, brings with it tremendous responsibility in that it is two-dimensional. Love has not only a vertical dimension (God's love for us and ours for Him); it also has a horizontal aspect (our love for those about us). Forgiveness, Jesus says, depends on our ability to forgive. You will be measured by the same yardstick you yourself use. As freely we received we must freely give. Thus, the fruit of the Spirit is love.

The writer of each epistle in the Bible emphasizes the importance of horizontal love. Paul states, "The greatest of these is love." Again, "Love is the fulfilling of the law." Peter adds, "Above all things have fervent love among yourselves." John claims, "God is love," and adds, "We know that we have passed from death unto life, because we love the brethren. He that loveth not his brother abideth in death."

Love, however, is a broad word. To some people, it is that sticky and selfish affection one experiences in adolescence. To another, it is that silly and flabby Santa Claus love demanding no discipline or withholding. Others feel it to be an unbending discipline allowing for no mistakes, much less human feeling. Therefore, it is necessary to define the kind of love which is the fruit of the Spirit.

Paul cogently clarifies the concept of love in his letter to Corinth. The ingredients of love are in a package and not a list from which we select ones appealing to us. One who truly loves is filled with all of these qualities and expresses them to all those about him. Love, Paul says, is patient, kind, generous, humble, courteous, unselfish, good tempered, guileless, and sincere.

Love defined is the first step. Love applied is the next. We must be careful not to glibly say we love. Rather, we need to analyze carefully all of life, applying each of Paul's ideals to see if we indeed do love. Generally, we have few problems in loving our friends and brothers in Christ. However, there are two aspects of life we often overlook when we think of ideal Christ-like love: love in the home and love in the world. Using Paul's yardstick of ideal Christian love, it would be wise to measure our lives in these areas to see if we do love first.

The Undivorced—Love in the Home

During a battle in Vietnam, two young men were in the thick of the fight with bullets flying about, shrapnel

19

bursting overhead, and occasionally a grenade exploding nearby. One of the young men, terrified by the situation, gasped, "Isn't this awful?"

The other replied, "Oh, not really. It just reminds me of home."

A prominent psychiatrist observed recently that while one out of three marriages ends in divorce, another one out of three is not so much a state of marriage as it is simply of being "undivorced." Love and communication are gone, but the couple remains together because of social pressures, children, finances, or some other reason. Tragically, the home degenerates into a battlefield of individual rights, sometimes noisy, sometimes silent, but always tense. The home becomes merely a house where an assortment of human beings just happen to eat and sleep together. From these situations come juvenile delinquents, neurotics, or worse. Unhappiness breeds unhappiness, and the children's marriages are often as chaotic as their parents'.

As a pastor I have seen similar circumstances in homes where both mates are members of the church and each feels he is following Christ. Invariably, there are deep spiritual problems, and it is clearly evident the fruit of the Spirit is lacking in these lives. Each points to the other, accusing of spiritual immaturity, when in actuality both are to blame. It is true, individuals mature at different rates, but regardless of the spiritual development of one, this should not determine the reaction of the other. Booker T. Washington said, "I will not permit any man to diminish my soul to hatred." Regardless of another's *action*, our *reaction* must reflect the fruit of the Spirit. Therefore, it would be wise to ask without consideration of our mate's personality, faults, or weaknesses, "Do *I* express the fruit of the Spirit in my marriage?" Am *I* patient, kind, generous, humble, courteous, unselfish, good tempered, guileless, sincere, regardless of my mate's action or reaction?"

Most of us would have to give a negative answer to these questions. Yet, such love is the fruit of the Spirit. Lest we despair, there is a way to cultivate this love in the home. God has given some excellent points to practice, until ideal love settles like a sweet mist in the home. These are active and must be put in practice. Peter lists them in his first epistle (1 Peter 3).

After setting the stage by saying that wives must be selfless and submissive, and that husbands must be honorable and loving, Peter lists some practical pointers for making love come alive. They sound so simple, yet they are so deeply profound.

"... *Be ye all of one mind.* . . ." The most common problem in marriage is lack of communication. Communication comes when we have one purpose and pleasure. Consequently, we must be like-minded. Those united in Christ are just this: their purpose and pleasure is to please Christ for His eternity. To them, marriage is not an end within itself, but a temporary association that brings great peace and joy to a human heart. Their possessions are really His and they merely use them for a moment. Thus, the many marriage problems of others are eliminated, not by refusal to handle them, but by relegating them to their proper importance. Problems with money, raising of children, sex, and in-laws are dealt with effectively as the common purpose and pleasure of both partners is kept in mind. These people learn to love deeply because eternal values are foremost.

"... *Having compassion one of another.* . . ." Compassion is defined as "sympathetic consciousness of another's distress, coupled with the desire to relieve it." Often, married couples in the heat of arguments, concentrate on one another's faults rather than on the problem. Because of this, the original problem is seldom solved, but is pushed back into the subconscious to join other unsolved problems. This leads not to relief, but frustration. It is wise to remember that the true definition of compassion is not only understanding the other's dis-

21

tress, but also desiring to relieve that distress. Each should strive to be the first to give a friendly sign, to nod first, smile first, speak first, and forgive first. Real strength is the ability and desire to tear down the invisible wall between mates that was built by misunderstanding.

" . . . *Love as brethren.* . . ." Strange words these appear to be! However, when one realizes the heart of Peter's message is the appeal for respect of each other in the marriage relationship, this phrase becomes understood. Are husbands and wives to have the same affection for one another as brothers in the Lord? How does this work? We do not speak disrespectfully to our brother in the Lord, lest he be offended. We are careful not to take advantage of him, and are quick to help him when he is in trouble. We make an effort to see that he enjoys the time he spends with us and that we favorably impress him. We are careful to not lose our temper in his presence.

Peter encourages married couples to have the same respect for each other as they do for their brothers and sisters in the Lord. It is easy to see how deeper, richer, and fuller our married love would be if we practiced loving as brethren. It is a beautiful thing to see a husband and wife, not only married, but also dearest friends.

" . . . *Be pitiful.* . . ." The New English Bible translates this, "be kindly." God did not create male and female alike psychologically, because each is to complement the other. Men feel and think differently than women, and often, it is hard to bridge that gap with kindness. Try as we will, we can never change their thinking and actions to those of ours. Deep frustration and inner conflict follow when we try. Here is where kindness comes in. Kindness is accepting the other person for what he is and loving him for that. Someone has said, "We like someone *because;* we love someone *although.*"

Too often I have seen those who have tried to change their whole psychological being to the desire of their mate, only to be rejected, because that mate did not really want what he thought he did. The point is that we should strive to be *better*, but never *different*. We run into severe problems when we try to become something we are not. It would be wise to remember, "It is the Lord who hath made us, not we ourselves." It is the wise mate who realizes his mate is an individual whom God has created not to be forced into an unnatural pattern bent to the sordid desires of the other mate. By being kind we can learn to appreciate and love that very different human being God has given us. "Love," a man said, "is the passionate and abiding desire on the part of two or more people to produce together conditions under which each can be, and spontaneously express, his real self; to produce together an intellectual soil and an emotional climate in which each can flourish, far superior to what each could achieve alone."

". . . *Be courteous: Not rendering evil for evil, or railing for railing: but contrariwise blessing.*" Here is one of the most important keys for a successful marriage. Marriage is not only *selecting* the right mate, but also *becoming* the right mate. Some wives complain their husbands are courteous and considerate in public, but rude and selfish at home. Similarly, husbands say wives are gracious and vivacious in a crowd, but moody and unkempt at home. Peter states that the simple courtesies extended to those about us should be found at all times in the home.

Too often, when we are hurt by our mate, we wish to hurt in return. When a mate speaks harshly, there is great temptation to respond in the same tone. However, Peter talks of oil on troubled waters when he encourages good for evil and softness for hardness. In marriage, more than any other place in life, there must be the willingness to go the second mile, turn the other cheek. We are to be thermostats, not thermometers, *affecting* the environment, not just reflecting it.

". . . *That your prayers be not hindered.* . . ." Here is a word of warning. The little war in Korea took as many lives as did Hiroshima. In like manner, the little wars in

23

our homes kill our families and threaten our societies. Also, misunderstanding in the home hampers our access to God. Our prayers can be blocked because we do not love. Therefore, it is imperative, not just convenient, that the fruit of the Spirit, love, reign in our hearts, and homes, lest we find we cannot pray, cannot get forgiveness, and therefore, cannot possess eternal life. The fruit of the Spirit is love in the home.

The Race of Death—Love in the World

Twenty-eight cars came roaring around the curve when something went wrong. Young David McDonald's car spun out of control and as he fought to right it, driver Eddie Sachs smashed into the side of the racer at one hundred-fifty miles per hour. An explosion ripped steel and rubber; fire spewed fifty feet in the air. One driver died in the wreckage and the other died two hours later in a hospital.

Three hundred thousand people watched in stunned silence and shocked sadness as death dropped its pall over the festive activities. The 1964 Memorial Day race was delayed for over an hour and forty-five minutes while crews raked up wreckage. Later, the race went on.

Many who watched or listened to the broadcast descriptions of the race later noted that the most significant thing to them was the fact that the race went on. This is a commentary on our times and brings home the tragic truth that we live in a highly impersonal world. Most of us only care about ourselves. Grief is but for a moment and we again take up the activity of living. William Cullen Bryant so eloquently penned:

> The gay will laugh
> When Thou art gone, the solemn brood of care
> Plod on, and each one as before will chase
> His favorite phantom.

While we are aware life continues and does not come to a halt with the loss of a loved one, still we must realize that we humans are growing farther apart. The supermarket has replaced the corner grocery store. The traditional drugstore where the gang met is now a discount center with clerks we do not recognize or wish to know. We have become numbers, statistics, ratings, and shiny credit cards.

One reason life has become so impersonal is the alarming population explosion. At the time of Christ there were about 300 million people on the earth; by 1700, approximately 625 million; by 1900, 1.6 billion; by 1950, 2.5 billion; by 1982, 4.6 billion. With this burgeoning population has come a decreasing importance of the individual. The pace of automation and computerization in industrialized countries has helped to reduce the individual to a mere number among millions of others.

Increasing with equal rapidity—or even faster—are emotional and mental breakdowns. The proportion of the population in mental institutions has skyrocketed since the turn of the century. Asked for an explanation, psychologists say it is because the individual is losing his identity, his importance. The world has become so impersonal it is driving itself crazy. Neighbors are no more. Men draw up on their own tight little islands and do not know how to cope with problems of an impersonal society.

Recently, the press carried a heartrending story of a young father who shot himself in a tavern telephone booth. James Lee had called a Chicago newspaper and told a reporter he had sent the paper a manila envelope outlining his story. The reporter frantically tried to trace the call, but was too late. When the police arrived, the young man was slumped in the booth with a bullet through his head.

In his pockets they found a child's crayon drawing, much folded and worn. On it was written, "Please leave in my coat pocket. I want to have it buried with me." The drawing was signed in childish print by his blonde daughter, Shirley Lee, who had perished in a fire just five months before. Lee was so grief stricken he had asked total strangers to attend his daughter's funeral so she would have a nice service. He said there was no family to attend since Shirley's mother had been dead since the child was two.

Speaking to the reporter before his death, the heart-broken father said that all he had in life was gone, and he felt so alone. He gave his modest fortune to the church Shirley attended and said, "Maybe in ten or twenty years, someone will see one of the plaques and wonder who Shirley Ellen Lee was and say, "Someone must have loved her very, very much." The grieving father could not stand loneliness or the loss, so he took his own life. He felt it better to be dead than live in an impersonal world.

Immediately, our hearts are moved by such an incident and we readily respond, "I would have shown love and tenderness to this man." However, the tragic truth is these lonely people do not wear signs making them identifiable. They are disguised behind expressionless faces, ragged rum-stained beards, and happy masks as fake as that of a circus clown. They are locked in their loneliness because they do not know how to break out of that prison. The only escape they know is at the bottom of a bottle, at the end of a blunt, drug-stained needle, or inside the shiny jacket of a barbiturate. We pass them each day and don't really see them. We are either awed or appalled by their veneer. We fail to see the lonely soul inside. Few of us know how to love the masses.

Jesus could look on a multitude and be moved with compassion for them. He could walk the lonely hillside at night, watching the sleeping city and weep for it. The miracle of His love is that He loved the masses and millions yet unborn so much He would die for them. His love knew not just the dimension of the small Judean countryside, but transcended all borders and ages. Consequently, He spent His waking hours making people happy and relieving them of their deep oppressions. Later, He would speak through His apostle saying that the fruit of this Spirit is love.

Love that is of the Spirit must relate to our lives. If we have this fruit, it means the nine ingredients Paul mentions in his love chapter. Love, such as Christ had, knows no race or faces. Perhaps we could pray God would expand our borders until we have this type of love. Too often, we judge a race, nation, or group of people, by their lowest expressions. However, real love is evaluating them by their highest ideals. The real Christian cannot express any racial or religious bigotry, be it silent or vocal, subtle or harsh. Real love that is the fruit of the Spirit is the love Christ showed toward mankind.

Granted, it is difficult to read of those far off and feel affection for them. God alone can help us develop such concern. However, while waiting for this ideal we can do some very practical things where we live to pay our debt of love to mankind. We can watch for broken hearts, be interested in the heartache of others rather than being wrapped up in our own small lives. This is the first step. Then, unseen deeds of charity and kindness are natural expressions of love. You may give without loving, but you cannot love without giving. Through personal involvement in your church's missionary program, charitable organizations, and gospel missions, you extend this love God gives. Dedicating your life to acts of love is following in Jesus' footsteps. When we do so, it would be wise to remember this little poem:

> I did a favor yesterday,
>   A kindly little deed . . .
> And then I called to all the world
>   To stop and look and heed.
> They stopped and looked and flattered me
>   In words I could not trust,
> And when the world had gone away
>   My good deed turned to dust.
>
> A very tiny courtesy
>   I found to do today;
> 'Twas quickly done, with none to see,
>   And then I ran away . . .

But Someone must have witnessed it,
　　For—truly-I-declare—
As I sped back the stony path
　　Roses were blooming there.

The fruit of the Spirit is love, and it sets the pace for all other fruit that follows. How can we have joy, peace, long-suffering, or the others without first being saturated thoroughly with the same love Christ knew? When we learn this love and express it, there is a beauty that comes to life we never knew before. In the beautiful poem, "Sella," Poet Bryant expresses this thought:

Her days henceforth were given to quiet tasks of good
　　In the great world. Men hearkened to her words,
And wondered at their wisdom and obeyed,
　　And saw how beautiful the law of love
Can make the cares and toils of daily life.

3

Thirst for Truth

Terror struck with fiery fangs that April morning in 1906 when the San Andreas Fault settled, shaking San Francisco to the ground. While thousands of panic-stricken refugees struggled to get out of the burning city, a man with rumpled hair, keen eyes, and a hawk-like nose rode into the city on the only train to reach it that day. He was William James, the famous psychologist who was then in his sixty-fourth year and suffering from a severe heart condition.

For the next twelve hours James scrambled amid roaring flames, falling buildings, and piled rubble, notebook in hand, eagerly asking fleeing inhabitants, "How did you feel when the shaking began?" "What thoughts flashed through your mind?" he asked. "Did your heart beat faster?" This was the passion and drive that made William James one of the foremost scientists of his generation. His thirst for truth caused him to explore, experiment, change and grow. He had an insatiable curiosity to learn about every facet of the human personality and all he could about the great secrets of life.

Tragically, the difference between scientists like William James and some religionists is that the scientist openly admits he does not possess all of truth and passionately seeks for it, while some religionists sit smugly claiming they have the answer to all of life's problems. Because of this attitude, some thinking people have looked upon religion as arrogant ignorance and there is very little in it that seems appealing. It doesn't take a genius to know there are many unanswerable problems to life and even Paul admits, "We see through a glass darkly."

Perhaps it is time we understand the really religious man is not one who sits in a high tower pouring wisdom down like beads from a broken string, but is like the scientist, passionately seeking for new insights, truths, and revelation. The only difference is the man who knows God has discovered the true path on which to walk in his search. But it is only a path, and to learn truth this man must walk and seek. God merely places us in the right direction much like a lost man given a compass in the deep of the forest. There is the proper sense of direction, but he still must walk his way out.

This premise is particularly important when it comes to understanding joy as the fruit of the Spirit. We must be realistic and recognize that there are some sincere Christians who have little joy in their souls. And, there are those who are not Christians, yet have very real bursts of joy. Our thirst for truth can drive us to seek the answer to this paradox. The observations that follow are mere suggestions that I hope will nudge us closer to understanding Paul's claim, "The fruit of the Spirit is joy." They do not pretend to be pat answers or a magic formula.

Joy is like a well containing sweet water. It is not enough to know the water is there or even to drill the well. If the well is to be useful, the water must be brought to the surface. Those who know Christ have found the source of joy, but some have not drawn from the well and therefore, their joy remains buried. Then, those who have no connection with God often feel bursts of joy, a melting into the universe, a real kinship with nature, an exultation of spirit. Psychologist Abraham Maslow observed these times in his patients and made a survey, reporting, "moments of great awe; moments of the most intense happiness or even rapture, ecstacy or bliss." He decided this was not necessarily a religious experience, but merely an expression of good health. Perhaps such moments are God's times of trying to break through man's veneer, exposing to him the larger and richer life.

There Is a River

Joy would seem like an elusive, fleeting thing, just beyond man's grasp. Joy is much more than happiness. It is "exultation of spirit," says the dictionary, "gladness; delight; a state of felicity." As Ardis Whitman says, "Awe and a sense of mystery are part of it; so are the feelings of humility and gratitude. Suddenly we are keenly aware of every living thing—every leaf, every flower, every cloud, the mayfly hovering over the pond, the crow cawing in the treetops." Professor Maslow said, "You cannot seek these moments directly. You must be 'surprised by joy.'" However, one can tap the reservoir and find continuous joy. Paul says, "The fruit of the Spirit is joy."

Early in man's history the psalmist said, "There is a river, the streams whereof shall make glad the city of God." Not only does he say there is a source; he goes on: "Thou wilt show me the path of life; in thy presence is fulness of joy; at thy right hand there are pleasures for evermore" (Ps. 16:11). Thus, we learn the source of the fullness of joy is the presence of God. It is then easy to see why the Spirit-filled believer would have great joy. God is with him and dwells in him so there is complete, continuous, and abiding joy.

After Scripture identifies the true source of joy, it reaffirms this truth over and over. A single characteristic of Jewish worship was great joy. In fact, the reputation of joy had so spread that when the Babylonians captured Israel they taunted them by saying, "Sing us one of the

31

joyful songs of your country." The Book of Acts talks about people being filled with joy and the Holy Ghost. The redeemed made melody in their hearts. After the Samaritan city received salvation, "There was great joy in the city." Paul says without apology, "The Kingdom of God is not meat and drink but righteousness, and peace, and joy in the Holy Ghost" (Rom. 14:17).

Recent archaeological discoveries uncovered letters written by martyrs during those first three trying centuries following Christ. Just before death one saint penned, "In a dark hole I have found cheerfulness; in a place of bitterness and death I have found rest. While others weep I have found laughter, where others fear I have found strength. Who would believe that in a state of misery I have had great pleasure; that in a lonely corner I have had glorious company, and in the hardest bonds perfect repose. All these things Jesus has granted me. He is with me, comforts me and fills with joy. He drives bitterness from me and fills me with strength and consolation."

I have stood in the prison where Paul was confined just before his martyrdom. The walls are cold, rough rocks; the dungeon is so damp one feels chilled at midday. Only a tiny hole lets in light and air. There is no heat, and the ceiling is so low I could not stand up straight. Paul stayed here at least two years and from here he wrote his last great epistle, Second Timothy. Although now electrically lighted, the tiny cell still seemed to close in on me.

That night I read again Paul's last letter to young Timothy. I noted there is not a word of melancholy, but it is shot through with triumphant rejoicing. Paul concludes, "I have fought a good fight, I have finished my course, I have kept the faith: Henceforth there is laid up for me a crown of righteousness, which the Lord, the righteous judge, shall give me at that day" (4:7, 8). There is a joy transcending trouble, leaping over walls of circumstances, and abiding through death. Paul does not speak of "bursts of joy," or "moments when it slips on us," but rather of a lasting, ever abiding, enduring exultation of spirit. "The fruit of the Spirit is joy." In John 7:38, 39 we find this promise of Jesus: "He that believeth on me, as the scripture hath said, out of his belly shall flow rivers of living water. (But this spake he of the Spirit, which they that believe on him should receive: for the Holy Ghost was not yet given; because that Jesus was not yet glorified.)"

The Sweet Here and Now

The foregoing description sounds idealistic; yet we know there are those who have attained this continuous and abiding joy. If this is so, why do we live so far beneath the level of this abiding joy? Perhaps it is because too often we program ourselves to live in the sweet bye and bye rather than in the right now. Sir William Osler admonished his patients to live in "daytight" compartments, dealing with the frustrations and joys of the right now. Longfellow warns:

> Trust no future, how ere pleasant.
>   Let the dead past bury its dead.
> Act, act in the living present,
>   Heart within and God o'er head.

It is too easy to borrow from tomorrow's sunshine and tuck away small joys of the present, anticipating keener ones tomorrow. Because we do not savor the little joys, the small pleasures, the minute delights, we miss much of life and God. Jesus asks that we be faithful over a few things and God would make us ruler over many.

Nursery rhymes often have a way of piercing the armor of human pretension, exposing our weakness for what it is. Dick Whittington's cat who went to London to see the queen is a case in point.

Pussy cat, pussy cat, what did you there?
I frightened a little mouse under her chair.

A lot of people are like that cat. In the splendor of the palace, the majesty of royalty, and the beauty of pomp, the poor cat could only see a mouse. Our lives are spent among the splendors of creation, yet so often we shuffle through life hardly lifting our eyes to the glories about us. Some have found the joy of living, but too many have settled for monotony of existence. Robert Louis Stevenson rightly said, "To miss the joy is to miss all."

There always seem to be legitimate reasons for our missing small joys around us. The other night I was rocking my little girl to sleep. She was busily chatting away, to my frustration. I wanted her to hurry and get to sleep because there were so many things I needed to get done. There were sermons to prepare, articles to write, calls to make, and letters that just had to get out. Inwardly, I resented this intrusion on my time. Just then she looked up and said simply, "Daddy, I love you."

It hit me hard. How callous I had been! Here was one of the most precious and joyous experiences of life and I was wishing it over, so I could "get things done." I whispered a prayer asking God's forgiveness, held my little girl close to me, and wished that moment could last forever.

A giant floral clock in St. Louis has the inscription, "Hours and flowers soon fade away." How true! Time is an enemy stealing from us the little but lofty moments of joy which deepen our souls' channels, carrying us nearer to God. Just as Christ healed the blind beggar, often we need Him to remove scales from our eyes so we might recognize the little joys and meaningful moments God brings our way each day.

Helen Keller said wisely, "Use your eyes as if tomorrow you would be stricken blind." She, blind these many years, said that if she had only three days to see, on the first day she would want to see the people whose kindnesses and companionship had made her life worth living. She would call in all her friends and look long at their faces. She would also look into the face of a baby. She would like to see the many books that have been read to her, and to look into the eyes of her dogs, faithful and loyal. She would take a long walk in the woods.

On the second day, Miss Keller said she would get up early to see the dawn. She would visit museums to learn of man's progress upward. She would also visit an art museum to probe man's soul by studying his pictures and sculptures. Then, at night she would visit the theatre to see the grace of the great ballerina Pavlova.

On the last day she would again be up to see the dawn, to discover new revelations of its beauty. Then she would visit the haunts of men, where they work. She would stand on the busy street corner, trying to understand something of the daily lives of people by looking into their faces and reading what is written there. She would also want to see suffering to feel compassion. She would like to tour New York, seeing the slums, the factories, the parks, and children at play.

On the last evening she would like to see a funny play to appreciate the overtones of comedy in the human spirit. The interesting thing to note is her desire to see the common things about us, and from this great woman we can learn to use our eyes and see the world about us. Somehow, if we could learn to see God's world, perhaps we could learn to see God, who indeed is the source of all joy.

Oh, that God could break through our lives until we are keenly aware of the soft smothering snow, the patter of persistent rain, the whispers of the wind. We need to be reminded that God not only promises to meet us in His sanctuary, but that He displays His handiwork everywhere in the world: "For the invisible things of him from the creation of the world are clearly seen, being understood by the things that are made, even his eternal power and Godhead" (Rom. 1:20).

But perhaps you are one who does not particularly like soft snowy fields and swirling rain-filled ditches. Maybe you don't get all choked up over a walk in the forest. The point is not to make a nature-lover of you, but merely to get you to open your eyes to the majesties God places around us. Robert Frost could look at a forest and be inspired to great poetry. Similarly, Carl Sandburg could see a bleak and busy Chicago and note a raw and rare beauty. Each saw beauty in two very different things, but both were inspired. Pablo Picasso could see his classic art piece, "The Bull's Head," in a broken bicycle. Michelangelo could feel Moses trying to burst forth in all fury from a marble slab. The important thing is not that we thrill to what other men do, but that we see and thrill.

War prisoners often come back relating terrible experiences during their captivity. Inevitably, they say they never really learned to appreciate food until they were without it. I always remember the prisoner who was given only a piece of stale cheese and bread a day. In his diary he described the exotic tastes and pleasures of that simple food. So many of us do not have joy because we never really have learned to live, to see, to feel, to act, in the living present. Jesus asks that we take no thought of tomorrow, but consider today. Edna St. Vincent Millay cried, "O world, I cannot hold thee close enough." If we really saw, really felt, really loved, really enjoyed what God has given us there would be this great out-pouring of joy in us.

A Walk with Destiny

However, full appreciation of the delights of today is not the complete answer. If so, then the humanist could carry us far enough. There are days when physical pain prevents us from keen appreciation of the pleasures about us. Tragedy stalks into our lives unannounced, tearing from us someone very dear. Circumstances weigh on us until our eyes are too heavy to hope. There must be something deeper and more meaningful if joy is to remain during trying times. There is—when we realize we are entities for eternity. Each one of us has his individual walk with destiny.

Imprisonment, disaster, and defeat could not conquer the plucky Englishman who in later years would be known as the "man of the century." During the Boer War, Winston Churchill was jailed in Pretoria, South Africa, but later escaped. Years passed and as first lord of the admiralty, he was personally blamed for the costly Dardanelles disaster and forced to resign. Even after successfully steering his nation through another war, his countrymen rejected him at the polls. Yet, he remained undaunted and rose again to be prime minister. He died the most esteemed man of his generation.

To understand Churchill's indomitable spirit which drove him to build again and again from the ashes of adversity, one only need read his writings. Speaking of that hour when circumstances of war thrust him to the front of world leadership, he said, "I was conscious of a profound sense of relief. At last I had the authority to give directions over the whole scene. I felt as if I were walking with Destiny, and that all my past life had been but a preparation for this hour and for this trial." These were not the idle words of an egocentric leader, but the deep conviction of a man who felt God had selected him to save England. History records the results of that conviction.

There are men who seem to grasp the fact that they are walking with destiny. They are the Churchills, Abraham Lincolns, and Ben-Gurions. What these men feel in the temporal is but a shadow of the eternal. All who are in Christ walk daily with Destiny. At eighteen Jeremiah trembled as God's finger wrote into his soul, "Before I formed thee in the belly I knew thee and before thou camest forth out of the womb I sanctified thee, and I ordained thee a prophet unto the nation" (Jer. 1:5).

Men of destiny suffer the same, and sometimes more, setbacks and frustrations that plague all men. The difference is that they know there is an *ultimate* scheme of things and a master plan. Therefore, the pains and problems of the present do not seem as important to them. They maintain their "Invictus" spirit in the full face of failure.

As humans we often misunderstand the meaning of destiny. To us life becomes an end within itself and the successes or failures of now are looked upon as ends within themselves.

Our problems center in the fact that we lose our perspective. When tragedy stalks, death comes, or failure consumes our ambitions, there is the temptation to lose sight of the eternal. Yet, it was this sight of the eternal that was the key to the great joy of the apostles. According to tradition, eleven of them died martyrs, with only John closing his eyes in natural death. Paul, speaking for all the apostles, could say, "These little troubles (which are really so transitory) are winning for us a permanent, glorious and solid reward out of all proportion to our pain. For we are looking all the time not at the visible things, but at the invisible. The visible things are transitory; it is the invisible things that are really permanent" (2 Cor. 4:17, 18). He knew we do not live for the paltry seventy years of earthly life, but are creatures of eternity.

Earlier in this letter to the Corinthians, Paul states that because his eyes are on the eternal, the immediate problems can be relegated to their proper place. "We are handicapped on all sides," Paul said, "but we are never frustrated; we are puzzled, but never in despair. We are persecuted, but we never have to stand it alone: we may be knocked down but we are never knocked out" (2 Cor. 4:8, 9, Phillips). But, lest we merely set our goals on that eternal life and just "suffer" through this one, he adds, "As long as we are clothed in this temporary dwelling we have a painful longing, not because we just want to get rid of these 'clothes' but because we want to know the full cover of the permanent house that will be ours . . . it is our aim, therefore, to please him whether we are 'at home' or 'away'" (5:4, 9). Paul was no suffering saint merely moping through life until God delivered him. Rather, he was a joyful, exuberant, vital child of God who could not be stopped by kings, priests, jails, or beatings. He was a man overtaken by the joy of God's presence.

It is vitally important that man believes in the ultimate purpose of creation. As a famous preacher once noted, "If irreligion were only disbelief in religion, we might stand it; but thoroughgoing irreligion—reducing the universe to protons and electrons, going it blind; no God behind it nor spiritual purpose in it—is not disbelief in religion alone, but fundamental disbelief in life itself." He further observed that the logical result of such skepticism would make people think, "What is the use anyway?" And the psychological result would be personal cynicism. Carl Jung, the noted Swiss psychologist, once had a patient tell him, "If I only knew that my life had some meaning and purpose, then there would be no silly story about my nerves." Human personality cannot flourish on any such futilitarian idea of life.

Thus, the seed of joy is sown by the Spirit and as we recognize the source of joy, keep our spirits receptive to His often tiny voice in things around us and keep our perspective by remembering we are creatures of destiny. Joy will grow in our lives until we know the thrill of not just snatched moments of joy, but the continuous and flooding river welling up and spilling over from our lives. This is Paul's fruit of the Spirit, joy. Finally, a reminder:

> There is nothing I can give you which you have
> not, but there is much that while I cannot
> give you, you can take.
> The gloom of the world is but a shadow;
> Behind it, yet within reach, is joy. Take Joy.

The fruit of the Spirit is . . .   **peace**

4

Worse than War

A shower of shots splattered the sunny afternoon with a Berliner's blood as he tried to vault over the infamous wall. For forty-five agonizing minutes he pleaded with East Berlin police to get him down from the wall and secure a physician's help. Stoically they stood with trained guns as slowly his life bled from him. This is the peace of Berlin.

There are many kinds of peace in the world. Walking along that Berlin wall one can feel the guards' eyes bore into one's back. There is a terrible tension there, a state of affairs in many respects worse than war. Yet, one would have to say there is absence of declared war and so this is a certain type of peace.

The peace of Auschwitz was a peace of death. Hitler tried to make peace with the Jews by exterminating them in his ghastly gas chambers, his "final solution." There has been the peace of slavery and subjection such as the Romans forced on their subjects. Today we are aware of communist countries in which there is an enforced peace.

Again, there is the peace of the tranquilizer and the highball, the peace of the "mainliner" and the drunk.

There is the peace of those withdrawn in mental institutions and of the "brainwashed" prisoners. But, as Winston Churchill so aptly said, "There are many things worse than war. Slavery is worse than war. Dishonor is worse than war." And, most peace known in the world today is worse than war. Or, at best, it is artificially induced and temporary. Longfellow echoed our dismay a century ago:

> And in despair I bowed my head;
> "There is no peace on earth," I said,
> "For hate is strong
> And mocks the song
> Of peace on earth, good will to men!"

It seems we have reason to despair when we remember eighty-five percent of all history concerns itself with war. America's short history has been punctuated by various conflicts. Even John D. Rockefeller, Jr.'s grant of 8.5 million dollars to start the United Nations seems wasted as tensions still tear at the world's throat.

The Contradiction of Christ

Isaiah with keen anticipation says, ". . . and his name shall be called Wonderful, Counselor, The mighty God, The everlasting Father, the Prince of Peace" (9:6). All Christian scholars agree this verse refers to Christ, the Child born and the Son given. Angels reflected this thought as they announced to shepherds, "Glory to God in the highest, and on earth peace, good will toward men" (Luke 2:14). Christ's disciples waited the fulfillment of these prophecies and then one day He staggered them with a troubling thought contrary to all they had read or heard. Jesus said, "Think not that I am come to send peace on earth: I came not to send peace, but a sword. For I am come to set a man at variance against his father, and the daughter against her mother, and the daughter in law against her mother in law. And a man's foes shall be of his own household" (Matt. 10:34-36).

A superficial understanding of peace would drive one to reason that there is contradiction in what was prophesied of Christ and what He said. However, a deeper search unlocks the mystery and pours profound truths into seeking hearts. God told Jeremiah, "See, I have this day set thee over nations and over the kingdoms, to root out, and to pull down, and to destroy, and to throw down, *to build, and to plant*" (1:10). Here is the formula. Before pure peace can come into a life there must be the rooting out, pulling down, destroying, throwing down of false ideals, gods, attitudes and thought processes. Such a maneuver, as Jesus predicted, would cause turmoil and tension.

Jesus further clarified the issue by saying a new garment is not sown on an old piece of cloth or new wine placed in old skins. Therefore, before peace can come there must be the transformation of character which Jesus termed the "new birth." Scripture warns and admonishes us that no man can serve two masters. A fountain cannot give forth both bitter and sweet water, and a tree can only produce one fruit. Paul pointedly asks, ". . . what fellowship hath righteousness with unrighteousness? and what communion hath light with darkness? And what concord hath Christ with Belial? . . ." (2 Cor. 6:14, 15).

Christ starts at the problem point and plugs the gaping hole in roiled minds, and builds again and plants with proper attitudes and ideals. Only after this does man know real peace. Peace is not just absence of conflict, withdrawal, a forced psychotic tranquility, but a deep abiding "rightness" inside that reflects that which is without. Luke's account of the angels' message is more properly interpreted, "Peace on earth among men of good will." Christ indeed is the Prince of Peace as those who know Him find this "rightness" inside and the good will that results. History records some accounts of this

43

type of peace in play: King Alfred's attitude toward the Danes in 878, President Lincoln's sympathy for the South in 1865, and General MacArthur's treatment of the Japanese in 1945. This is peace on a world scale exercised through men of "good will" who had found inner peace.

Ultimately, when Christ's Kingdom comes, the world will see this peace in full sway. Until then we can exercise proper peace in our lives and be men of good will. James reminds us, "And the fruit of righteousness is sown in peace of them that make peace" (3:18). Paul says, "The fruit of the Spirit is peace." The peace that Christ gives is not just that found in pleasant circumstances, or in a stoical indifference to passion and feeling, or an epicurean freedom from pain, but a deep abiding tranquility in all circumstances and in all tension. There is a certain depth where the ocean remains calm despite howling winds driving at its surface or churning springs belching from the bottom. Similarly, there is a peace in Christ transcending troubles and this peace is the fruit of the Spirit.

Bringing Peace into Play

Defining peace does little good since diagnosis is more often easier than cure. However, the Bible not only talks about this peace which passes understanding but also offers practical advice on how to bring peace into play in our everyday life. These suggestions spread from the Bible's beginning to John's triumphant visions in The Revelation. Consideration of just a few of these aids is worthwhile.

Know God. Just as the source of true joy is God, so He is the source of peace. Eliphaz's eloquent speech in the Book of Job asserts, "Acquaint now thyself with him, and be at peace . . ." (22:21). Paul further clarifies the concept of peace in Ephesians 2:14: "For he [Christ] is our peace. . . ." Righteousness and "rightness" can only come from God; so there can only be peace in the heart when Christ has full control of the life.

Loving His law. The psalmist said centuries ago, "Great peace have they which love thy law: and nothing shall offend them" (119:165). In this age of skepticism it is easy to take God's Word lightly and regard it as irrelevant. However, timeless truths are hid in it which will help those caught in webs of any dilemma. Dr. Smiley Blanton, director of the American Foundation of Religion and Psychiatry, was once asked if he read the Bible. He replied, "I not only read it, I study it. It's the greatest textbook on human behavior ever put together. If people would just absorb its message, a lot of us psychiatrists could close our offices and go fishing." He went on to comment how foolish it is to not make use of the distilled wisdom of 3,000 years.

God's Word assures us of the ultimate "rightness" of things and that all things indeed work together for good. It sets down basic principles for peace such as, "underneath are the everlasting arms"; "love thy neighbor as thyself"; "take no thought of tomorow"; and "ye shall know the truth, and the truth shall make you free." Paul tells Timothy that Scripture is profitable, "That the man of God may be perfect . . ." (2 Tim. 3:17). There is peace in loving and living His Word. A familiarity with God's Word can help us to solve our problems, for the Bible contains many examples of men of the past who had similar problems, but were victorious in overcoming them.

Practice peace. Paul writes to the Colossians, "And let the peace of God rule in your hearts . . ." (3:15). To have peace and retain peace we must practice peace.

Psychologist William James said much about the truth of this admonition. He was one of the first psychologists who propounded the theory that every sensation, every contact with the outside world leaves a permanent trace among the ten billion brain cells. These traces are permanent and constantly accumulating and the sum total

45

of them is our personality and character. He went on to emphasize that everything we do makes it easier to do the same thing again. This is because the electrical currents record all that is happening and creates pathways among the brain cells. The more frequently any action is performed the deeper and broader these pathways become. James said, "The man who has daily inured himself to habits of concentrated attention, energetic volition and self-denial will stand like a tower when everything rocks about him and when his softer fellow mortals are winnowed like chaff in the blast. Sow an action and you reap a habit; sow a habit and you reap a character; sow a character and you reap a destiny."

His theory was further expounded as he said, "We are spinning our own fates, good or evil. Every smallest stroke of virtue or vice leaves its never-so-little scar. As we become drunks by so many separate drinks, so we become saints and authorities and experts by so many separate acts and hours of work." In other words peace can come into our lives by letting it rule in our lives and consciously acting upon the peace we now have. Continual peace, the peace of Christ, should sway our entire existence. We remain calm in tension, untroubled in trial, and determined in disaster. This was the peace of mind, heart, and character Jesus exhibited during the trying hours of ordeal at Calvary.

The Making of Men

Sometimes it is difficult to remain peaceful of mind and heart in times of turmoil. However, if we could realize there is an ultimate scheme of things and God is doing something most worthwhile in our lives there would be the calmness of spirit regardless of circumstances. God is trying to make men of us.

Born into the turbulence and strife of the fifteenth century was one of the greatest geniuses the world has ever known. His name was Michelangelo Buonarroti, and he was a master not only of painting, but of architecture, science, and above all, of sculpture. He felt chosen by God to wrest from stone great pieces of art which would seem to breathe with life.

Michelangelo often expressed the thought that for him art was not a science, but the "making of men." He considered stone a prison in which vital forms lived and his challenge was, "liberating the figure from the marble that imprisons it." Because of this genius, the world has such famous art pieces as *David*, *The Pieta*, *Moses*, and *The Bacchus*.

Michelangelo's drive to free forms from their stony prisons is but a shadow of the Great Artist, God, and His desire to make men. However, God does what no artist could ever do in that He does not just make the form of man, but breathes into him life and life more abundantly. The Great Sculptor speaks of carving the soul of man, "to be conformed to the image of his Son" (Rom. 8:29). God wrests from the stone of our human frailties and blatant inadequacies a vibrant image there imprisoned. He frees it by His power to live forever in the exhilarating air of His presence.

In several places in Scripture there is the picture of God as Master Artist toiling over His creation, molding and forming until He is satisfied with His work. This portrait of Jehovah must have been with Job as he penned, "Thine hands have made me and fashioned me together round about; yea thou dost not destroy me. Remember, I beseech thee, that thou hast made me as the clay" (Job 10:8, 9).

To some, this image of God may seem absurd. God seems too big to toil over a lump of clay or concern Himself with the tiny soul of a single man. However, Paul reaffirms, "Being confident of this very thing, that he which hath begun a good work in you will perform it until the day of Jesus Christ" (Phil. 1:6). If hearts still doubt His personal interest, one only need read the song of the psalmist which insists, "The Lord will perfect that which concerneth me; thy mercy, O Lord, endureth forever: forsake not the works of thine own hands" (Ps. 138:8).

Isaiah says much of the might and majesty of God. He speaks of nations being but a drop in the bucket compared to the power and providence of God. Isaiah saw the holiness of God as something so sacred he cries, "Woe is me! For I am undone: because I am a man of unclean lips." Yet, this same silver-tongued prophet said that God wrote into his soul, "Can a woman forget her sucking child, that she should not have compassion on the son of her womb? Yea, they may forget, yet will I not forget thee." To further assure a frail and fainting nation, God continues, "Behold I have graven thee upon the palms of my hands; thy walls are continually before me" (Isa. 49:15,16). God is the Master Sculptor concerned about the beauty of our lives.

Sculptors sometimes suffer failure when their stone prisons refuse to give up some essential part of their prisoners. Michelangelo felt this frustration when carving *St. Matthew*. Only half finished, this piece seems to suggest the struggle for liberation. However, Michelangelo could not wrench it free; he put down his tool in defeat. One could ask, "Couldn't the figure have been finished some way? Surely, there is enough material left for that?" He probably could have finished the statue, but not in the way he wanted, and in that case, the defeat would have been even more stinging. So, he stopped. Michelangelo left several unfinished statues, four of the most famous being the *Captive Giants* in Florence. In these works he had failed.

Is it possible that the stone of our lives is so marred or unyielding God would give up on us in His chiseling process? Jeremiah gives the answer to this in the poignant parable of the potter. Jeremiah is told to go to the potter who is busy making vessels. As he watched the nimble finger of the artist a crisis came, "And the vessel that he made of clay was marred in the hand of the potter: so he made it again another vessel, as seemed good to the potter to make it." Making sure Jeremiah understood the meaning, God says of Israel, ". . . cannot I do with you as this potter? saith the Lord. Behold, as clay is in the potter's hand, so are ye in mine hand" (Jer. 18:4-6).

While human artists sometimes fail because of the flaws in their material, God cannot fail, but will continue to mold vessels to His use. He has pledged Himself to success. So often we prove how marred we really are. David did, and Moses certainly showed very human and earthy traits. Yet, God patiently molds and makes these vessels to His likeness. David could confidently pray, "Have mercy upon me, *according to thy lovingkindness*: *according unto the multitude of thy tender mercies blot out my transgressions*" (Ps. 51:1). It is a great source of peace to hear the psalmist who sang, "He remembererd they were but flesh."

While the thought of being sculptured by God and having our flaws chipped away sounds good, yet, it hurts. We are not stone which yields without pain to the biting chisel. Some of the blows we receive may make us better, but they hurt deeply. The process of liberation is usually a long one, and it may prove extremely difficult for us. We cannot seem to understand why a certain illness is good for us even though the Word says, "He maketh me to lie down." The disappointment swallowing our ambition deadens our hopes and we did not know our Christian friends could or would hurt us so badly. One woman after losing her loved one cried, "Oh, I wish I had never been made." Her friend wisely replied, "You are not made, you are being made. This is part of the process." Every event, facet, and happening is part of God's cutting away process, "and we know that all things work together for good to them that love God" (Rom. 8:28). It's truth, but it still hurts. At times like these we need not just the Artist's blow, but also the Great Physician's touch.

One of the most beautiful pictures of Christ is that of Him healing broken men. Note that He touched them. He placed His hands on their eyes, on their fevered brows, on their throbbing limbs. And from that touch came healing, wiping away not only pain, but also remembrance of it. At the Last Supper He washed His disciples' feet. How often they must have thought of that moment when in later years they longed for His return.

Christ told of His Father's love in the story of the Prodigal Son. The father had every reason to be angry with the wayward boy. He had squandered his fortune and education. Yet, the father did not wait at the door with a prim word of welcome, or a reluctant handshake. Rather, watching eagerly, he saw his son afar off, ran and fell on his neck and kissed him. This is the healing touch.

David talks about this touch in his famous Shepherd's Psalm: "He restoreth my soul." Sheep in Palestine excel in the herding instinct. Each morning they start in their particular place in line and continue in it. However, sometime during the heat of the day each sheep will slip out of his place in line and trot over to the shepherd to receive a touch on the head, a scratch behind the ear. Satisfied that the shepherd loves it, the sheep goes back to the group with his "soul" restored. David adds clarity in the concluding verses: "He anointest my head with oil." At night the shepherd sat by the sheepfold door and examined each sheep as it came in. If one had been scratched or bruised he took healing salve and generously covered the wound. No wonder David could exclaim, "My cup runneth over."

It isn't always easy to be made over by God. However, whom the Son makes free is free indeed. When we have been liberated from the fleshly prison that binds us in frustration and failure, we become the great pieces of art God desires of us. We really learn to live! The Master Sculptor is working, and our prayer should echo that of Paul, ". . . always laboring fervently for you in prayers, that ye may stand perfect and complete in all the will of God" (Col. 4:12).

When the final history of this century is written it will probably be said we have sought more and found less peace than all generations before us. Sometimes peace is like putting kittens in a basket. You just get one in and another pops out. All over the world trouble spots erupt like putrid boils spewing forth violence and the pus of human atrocities.

Personal peace seems just as elusive. Men seek peace by self-explosion—drunkenness, sexual excess, drugs, and all the rest. Tragically, they, like the Persian poet Omar Khayyam, come out the same door in which they went. In this age the voice of real, vital, great religion needs to be sounded with clarion call so men might see the Prince of Peace. There is peace to be had, but it must be the pure and lasting peace of Christ.

Only after achieving a faith like this can we join Longfellow on his last verse of that famous Christmas carol:

> Then pealed the bells more loud and sweet
> "God is not dead nor doth He sleep.
> The wrong shall fail,
> The right prevail,
> With peace on earth, good will to men."

5

The Locust Years

For more than twenty years Robert Frost was a failure. He often said that during this time he was one of the very few persons who knew he was a poet. The world mourned his passing, and today he towers as one of America's greatest verse writers. His poems have been published in twenty-two languages, with his American edition alone selling over a record million copies. He was a four-time winner of the coveted Pulitzer Prize for poetry and had more honorary degrees thrust on him than probably any other man of letters.

Robert Frost was thirty-nine before he ever sold a volume of poetry. He had been writing for twenty years and received endless rejection slips. However, his perseverance paid off and the world is wiser and richer for it.

An eminent psychiatrist, Dr. George Crane, recently listed various ingredients for greatness. Among those he noted are the qualities we expect to see in such a list: talent, responsibility, and devotion to duty. Then, surprisingly, he said that physical stamina is also necessary. He reasons that many men do not reach the apex of their endeavors until late in life and therefore endurance is necessary. He cited Winston Churchill as a prime example.

What is true in the physical is certainly true in the spiritual. If we are to reach the ultimate in what God wants us to be, there must be spiritual endurance or stamina. Paul calls this fruit of the spirit, *longsuffering*, that which is best defined as endurance in all situations. Christ said, "But he that shall endure unto the end, the same shall be saved" (Matt. 24:13). The writer of the Book of Hebrews offered this truth: "For we are made partakers of Christ, if we hold the beginning of our confidence stedfast unto the end." (3:14). Later, he noted that Christ set the pace for endurance, "Who for the joy that was set before him endured the cross, despising the shame and is set down at the right hand of the throne of God" (12:2).

Some claim that preachers have made the Christian faith too easy, while others reply that Christ says His burden is light and His yoke easy. Paradox as it may be, both arguments are right. It is easy to let Christ live in you, but there is an eternal struggle. Paul points out, "For we wrestle not against flesh and blood, but against principalities, against powers, against the rulers of the darkness of this world, against spiritual wickedness in high places" (Eph. 6:12). In his last letter to Timothy, Paul admonishes, "Endure hardness as a good soldier of Jesus Christ" (2 Tim. 2:3). It is easy to serve Christ because, ". . . greater is he that is in you, than he that is in the world" (1 John 4:4). But, it is hard because, as Jesus told Peter, "Satan hath desired to have you that he may sift you as wheat" (Luke 22:31).

Driven to Despair

Wise in war, Satan does not concentrate on the big battles, but hammers away at our little struggles. Because we are expecting some great strife, some momentous attack from his quarters, we often fail to recognize the erosion of the buttress of our souls by his continued attacks in little things. A distraught woman handed me a poem one day, whispering to me that it described what had happened to her. I don't know the author, but I can testify to its truth.

> I thought, if defeat came at all,
> It would be in a big, bold
> Definite joust
> With a cause or a name.
> And it came.
>
> I had not thought the daily skirmish
> With a few details, worthwhile;
> And so I turned my back upon them
> Year on year; until one day
> A million minutia blanketed together
> Rose up and overwhelmed me.

Little things drive us to despair. Unresolved frustration, so small it seems silly, mounts up until we are blinded to the path before us. In these times we act and react out of character with our Christian testimony. This is what happened to a Texas minister who was scheduled to speak at an all-day conference. He was running late because his alarm had failed to ring. In his haste to make up for lost time he cut himself while shaving. Then he found his shirt was not ironed. To make matters worse, running to his car he noticed a tire was flat.

Disgusted, and by this time thoroughly distraught, the minister finally got underway with a sudden burst of speed. Racing through town he failed to notice a stop sign and rushed through it. As fate would have it, there was a policeman nearby, and in just moments he heard the scream of a siren.

Jumping out of his car, the agitated minister said sharply, "Well, go ahead and give me a ticket. Everything else has gone wrong today." The policeman walked up and said quietly, "Sir, I used to have days like that before I became a Christian."

Needless to say, the embarrassed minister was shamed by the stranger's rebuke and went his way asking forgiveness and praying for strength to correct his attitude.

We all have days when things just don't seem to go right. Even Christians are not free from the tensions of life that tear at our nerves. Christ never promised freedom *from* tension, but endurance *in* tension. If Satan can sap us of strength in these minute battles, his big battles are unnecessary.

When we ponder the story of the Texas minister our minds are thrust toward similar situations in our lives, when we have come up loser in one of these small but spiritual struggles with Satan. It would be wise to consider what can be done to prevent defeat in the future and to endure during these trying moments.

Someone left out a hyphen and it cost the U.S. government over $18,000,000. *Reader's Digest* reported the incident and said the hyphen was omitted when instructions were fed to a computer which was to guide a rocket to Venus.

A mass of coded information, fed to the machine, guided the rocket through the first phase of the flight. For an instant the computer and rocket lost touch. Although the rocket veered slightly off course, a hyphen—they call it a bar—in the instructions was to tell the rocket not to worry. There was no bar, and the rocket worried. The computer began sending course directions it should not have sent, and the rocket had to be destroyed.

Commenting on the incident the reporter said, "A touching and, in an odd way, a human story. The rocket was primed for a 180,000,000-mile trip, and stumbled over something this - long."

I like to think of prayer as the hyphen of our lives. It really does not involve a lot of time. The time of our prayers may be minutes rather than hours; it may consist of odd moments throughout the day. However, this small hyphen in our lives is that which tells us not to worry. If it is not there we worry and our lives are sometimes wrecked with frustration.

The best time to pray about a matter is the very moment it bothers you. If the minister would have taken time when he first got up to insert the hyphen of prayer in his day, he probably would have had a far different attitude. As it was, aggravation piled on aggravation until he exploded. If we could learn the secret of *instant access* to God our endurance during stress would be much greater.

Two hundred years ago a monk who washed pots and pans in a monastery gave us a priceless key to living. Brother Lawrence, who became well known not because of his brilliant theology, but because he lived so abundantly like Christ, wrote a booklet, *The Practice of the Presence of God*. He said, "The time of business does not with me differ from the time of prayer; and in the noise and clatter of my kitchen, while several persons are at the same time calling for different things, I possess God in as great a tranquility as if I were on my knees in blessed sacrament."

So here is the key: *instant access*. We must realize that Christ is with us every moment. At the point of frustration we must turn to Him for wisdom, strength, and grace. The songwriter was right:

> O what peace we often forfeit,
> O what needless pain we bear,
> All because we do not carry
> Everything to God in prayer.

Satan need not succeed in the small spiritual skirmishes if we hand the controls of our lives over to the One who overcame by the cross and desires to make us be overcomers by our lives.

The "Why" Question

Perhaps the greatest test of our endurance occurs when suffering almost smothers us and we are tempted to pose the "why" question. In the full face of affliction it is hard to see any sense to things that befall us and we want to question the fairness of a faithful God. However, these moments can be the most meaningful of our lives. The ancient prophet Joel quotes God, "I will restore to you the years that the locust hath eaten . . ." (Joel 2:25).

There are years in South Africa when locusts swarm the land and eat the crops. They come in hordes, blocking out the sun. The crops are lost and a hard winter follows. The "years that the locusts eat" are feared and dreaded. But the year after the locusts, South Africa reaps its greatest crops, for the dead bodies of the locusts serve as fertilizer for the new seed. And, the locust year is restored as great crops swell the land.

This is a parable of our lives. There are seasons of deep distress and afflictions that sometimes eat all the usefulness of our lives away. Yet, the promise is that God will restore those locust years if we endure. We will reap if we faint not. Although now we do not know all the "whys" we can be assured our times are in His hands. I feel there are at least three reasons God permits afflictions to come to His saints, and perhaps these could be considered with profit.

The first is *discipline*. Many years ago a young man lost his wife suddenly by a stroke. Later, he was stricken ill for a year and unable to move. Then he could not speak and suffered other heartaches. This was not an evil or irreligious man, but a godly man, who had dedicated his life to the ministry. Still, Ezekiel suffered. From the midst of his heartache he quotes God, "Can thine heart endure, or can thine hands be strong, in the days that I shall deal with thee? I the Lord have spoken it, and will do it" (22:14). Ezekiel knew well and communicated to Israel the fact that afflictions can come as discipline. His own life typified how God would deal with a wayward nation.

Although God forgave David's complicity with Bathsheba, yet punishment followed. Their illegitimate child died and the stain of war's blood never washed from his home. True forgiveness is forgiving the sinner, but not the sin. Punishment must follow because of the hurt to God, friends, and the sinner himself. Weak and ineffective parents who produce selfish and hateful children are tragic testimonies of forgiving both offender and offense.

Unfortunately, many do not recognize discipline when it comes. Speaking of David to Samuel, God said, "I will be his father, and he shall be my son. If he commit iniquity, I will chasten him with the rod of men, and with the stripes of the children of men" (2 Sam. 7:14). Often discipline comes in the form of sickness, sorrow, or some great disappointment.

Regardless of whether the affliction be human problems or illnesses, one would be wise to ask himself if it is righteous chastisement of God. Rather than resent such discipline we should welcome it and be better for it. J. B. Phillips translates Hebrews 12:5-13: "My son, regard not lightly the chastening of the Lord, nor faint when thou art reproved of Him; for whom the Lord loveth He chasteneth, and scourgeth every son whom He receiveth.

"Bear what you have to bear as 'chastening'—as God's dealing with you as sons. No true son ever grows up uncorrected by his father. For if you had no experience of the correction which all sons have to bear, you might well doubt the legitimacy of your sonship. After all, when we were children we had fathers who corrected us, and we respected them for it. Can we not much more readily submit to a Heavenly Father's discipline, and learn how to live.

"For our fathers used to correct us according to their own ideas during the brief days of childhood. But, God corrects us all our days for our own benefit, to teach us His holiness. Now obviously, no 'chastening' seems pleasant at the time; it is in fact, most unpleasant. Yet when it is all over, we can see that it has quietly produced the fruit of real goodness in the characters of those who have accepted it in the right spirit. So, take a fresh grip on life and brace your trembling limbs. Don't wander away from the path, but forge steadily onward. On the right path the limping foot recovers strength and does not collapse."

A second reason why God permits affliction to occur is that of *development*.

Not much happened during the eight-year presidency of James Monroe. Things were so peaceful historians dubbed the time as the "era of good feeling." However, James Monroe is not considered one of the great presidents. Historians agree the mark of a great president is how he reacts in crisis. Thus, Abraham Lincoln, George Washington, Woodrow Wilson, and sometimes F. D. Roosevelt are listed as great presidents. Strange, but true, tragedy, tension, and trials bring out the best in men.

Henry Ford was once asked to name his best friend. The auto magnate replied, "My best friend is the one who brings out the best in me." The Christian feels his best friend is Christ. However, we often fail to understand the implication of that friendship, His demands to bring out the best in us. Hence, we are often afflicted for our development.

Strange words appear in Psalm 119, "It is good for me that I have been afflicted; that I might learn thy statutes" (v. 71). And again, "I know, O Lord that thy judgments are right, and that thou in faithfulness hast afflicted me" (v. 75). These are not just rhyming words of an uninvolved poet, but the heart throb of a man longing for God's nearness. He knew God's afflictions draw men to the Creator. Paul pleaded, "That I may know him, and the power of his resurrection, and the *fellowship of his sufferings*, being made conformable unto his death . . ." (Phil. 3:10).

In the awesome and allegorical Song of Solomon there is a dialogue telling much of development in affliction. Speaking to the bride, the lover says, "A garden inclosed is my sister, my spouse; a spring shut up, a fountain sealed" (4:12). He goes on to say that within his love are beautiful spices of sweet smell. The bride replies, "Awake, O north wind; and come thou south; blow upon my garden, that the spices thereof may flow out" (v. 16). The Christian is a garden enclosed and often real spiritual beauty can only come when he yields to the winds of affliction.

Christ's prayer as well as the poignant prayer He taught His disciples were not pleas for pity or deliverance, but charged with, "Thy will be done." Sometimes one gets the feeling there are spiritual leaders who would deny saints of true development by insisting God will deliver them if they have faith and persistence. How different the attitude of the proverbist, ". . . feed me with food convenient for me . . ." (30:8).

Dietrich Bonhoeffer, himself a martyr many times before he died, said, "When Christ calls a man, he bids him come and die." Many fall at the feet of the cross in contrition, but there are others who seem to actually stretch themselves out on the cross and die with Christ. Paul was such a man. "I am crucified with Christ; nevertheless I live; yet not I, but Christ liveth in me . . ." (Gal.2:20). In another book he explains the sufferings of these select saints by saying, "We are made as the filth of the earth, and are the offscouring of all things unto this day" (1 Cor. 4:13). The lives of these men vividly remind us of the sheer beauty of a suffering life. God does send affliction for development of character and soul.

Direction can also be given as a reason why God sends affliction.

Sadness settled deeply in the soul of a young captive. His trek to Egypt by camel train was only a small part of the suffering Joseph would endure during his long and lonely exile. How could he know prison awaited him, betrayal by those he had helped, and separation from those he loved. If ever a man felt afflicted, it must have been this young son of Jacob.

In the cold light of history, one can see the wisdom of the affliction. If Joseph had not been sold into slavery, a nation could not have been preserved. If he had not suffered so at the hands of his brethren, he could not have known compassion for the suffering he showed. In retrospect, uninvolved emotionally, we can well see how God used affliction for direction in this lad's life.

Unfortunately, we are not as philosophical about our own situation as we are about Joseph's. In the passions of the present and the tears of our time we cannot see any sensible purpose in the affliction that is with us. However, we must remember we are walking through the valley of life walled about, not seeing the path before. There is One who stands far above this valley and knows the end from the beginning. Often, He detours us with affliction so His best possible good can be done. No wonder Job said, "But he knoweth the way that I take: when he hath tried me, I shall come forth as gold" (23:10).

History is filled with those who have not heeded God's direction in affliction. Saul refused to receive the affliction for direction and lost his anointing and the kingdom. Later, Solomon, a man of such great promise, turned his ear from the rumbles of affliction and in the latter years strayed from God. He had everything to make him happy, but somewhere lost his touch with God. God dealt through affliction, but he failed to respond. It must have been from his despair he wrote, "Sorrow is better than laughter: for by the sadness of the countenance the heart is made better" (Eccles. 7:3).

The songwriter has wisely said, "The way of the cross leads home." Crosses conjure up images of sacrifice and suffering. God does not promise padded pews or carpeted race tracks. His promise is to those who overcome. Because He loves His own and gave Himself for them He guides them often with affliction. These paths are not always easy, but they are still the shortest way home.

After a long life of affliction and learning to depend directly on God for direction, Paul writes, "For our light affliction, which is but for a moment, worketh for us a far more exceeding and eternal weight of glory . . . (2 Cor. 4:17). The hymnwriter says,

> The path that I have trod,
>   Has brought me nearer God,
> Tho' oft it led thro' sorrow's gates.
>   Tho' not the way I'd choose,
> In my way I might lose the joy
>   That yet for me awaits.

God does deal with His people in affliction for discipline, development and direction. James, who later was beaten to death for the Christ he loved said, "Blessed is the man that endureth temptation; for when he is tried, he shall receive the crown of life, which the Lord hath promised to them that love him" (James 1:12). Rather than whimper when afflictions come our way, rather than becoming spiritual paranoids when sickness strikes, we should remember God heals *people*, not *diseases*. Diseases are often only symptoms and Ezekiel queries if our hearts can stand when God deals with us. We should sing with the writer,

> Submission to the will of Him who guides me still
>   Is surely of His love revealed. My soul shall rise above
> The world in which I move; I conquer only where I yield.

The Man Who Came Back

David's endurance had stretched to a breaking point. For months he had been chased through parched desert by a mad king bent on murder. Bone-tired, he and his ragtag group of men came to their camp to find it burned and plundered. While they were away their families had been kidnapped and perhaps murdered. In their despairing anger they turned on David and spoke of stoning him. If he had not led them away on the last mission, this would not have happened.

In this soul-crushing moment the majesty of the man David springs forth. The Bible simply says, ". . . but David encouraged himself in the Lord his God" (1 Sam. 30:6). Driven to despair and the brink of disaster, he came back victorious with the knowledge that God who had led him before would not fail him now. The rest of the chapter tells how, under God's direction, he led the recapture of all their goods and their families. There was no loss of life.

The fruit of the Spirit is endurance and it is not always easy. However, in our moments of despair it would be well to remember that lonely figure long ago who encouraged himself in the Lord. Just as David knew deliverance would come, we rest assured our locust years will be restored. Habakkuk seems to capture the very heartbeat of God when he writes God's message, "But these things I plan won't happen right away. Slowly, steadily, surely, the time approaches when the vision will be fulfilled. If it seems slow, do not despair, for these things will surely come to pass. Just be patient! They will not be overdue a single day!" (Hab. 2:3, *Living Prophecies*).

6

The Tender Touch

Terror tightened the native's throat as he clutched his dying son and ran through the hot dust two miles to Africa's Baragwanath Hospital. Instinctively he knew it was too late and upon arrival had to sadly turn homeward with the baby cold in his arms. The child had died of gastric enteritis and tears dropped in the dirt as the sobbing father carried the lifeless form.

Vusamazulu Mutwa built the crude coffin and prepared his tiny son's body for burial. To a Bantu, proper burial is of vital importance. To be buried in an unknown grave or a pauper's grave is the deepest disgrace that can befall a Bantu anywhere in Africa. But the Bantu has no access to any cemetery unless he belongs to a recognized church and the funeral is presided over by a minister. A well-known authority has said, "Determination to have a proper burial is a strong reason why natives turn to Christianity."

The grief-stricken parents went to their "Christian" pastor, whose church the wife had attended many years; the father had never accepted the faith. When they asked for a funeral the pastor flatly refused, giving no reason for that denial. Later Mutwa acidly wrote, "Strangely, the

65

priest knew exactly what he was doing to me when he refused to bury my son, for over the years I had explained to him all the laws and customs of the Bantu. He refused simply because I was not, with the rest of my family, a member of his church."

From this tragic experience Vusamazulu Mutwa wrote a scorching essay on "Why Christianity Has Failed in Africa." It is part of his bitter book, *Africa Is My Witness*, which charges, "The culprits are those petty dictators and sadists who wear their white collars the wrong way round."

All of us in some small or large way have been burned by pharisaical and rigid religion which demands observance of a legal code without human compassion. Jess Moody has said, "God never called us to be dour judges, standing in the robes of prudery. We are in the business of redemptive involvement—not hyperrighteous investigation." He went on to say, "We must not be a terror for sinners, but a haven for them."

And the charge of unbending legalism cannot be made against just one church or organization. Even the most evangelical can become the whited sepulchers Jesus spits at with white-hot but holy anger. Paul settles forever the position we must take when he says, "The fruit of the Spirit is gentleness."

What Is God Like?

There is always one question I ask everyone who comes to my office seeking solutions to troubles that tear them. The question is, "What is the single quality that strikes you most about Christ?" Without exception they will say it is understanding, or tenderness, gentleness, or kindness. Then I remind them Jesus twice said, "If ye had known me, ye should have known my Father also . . ." (John 14:7).

It is true the "hellfire and brimstone" preacher can throw a thousand verses of Scripture at us, noting God's judgment and punishment. God did say flatly to Ezekiel, ". . . The soul that sinneth, it shall die" (18:4). However, God also said, "For the bread of God is he which cometh down from heaven, and giveth life unto the world" (John 6:33). The fact is God deals with a man in the direction he is going. The blatant and willful sinner will die. The seeking and sincere heart will find and be saved. Before we were ever part of the mystery called "time" the battle lines were already drawn. Satan's rebellion won for him everlasting abandonment and punishment. We will share that eternity with whichever master we choose. If we serve Satan we suffer his eternity. If we serve Christ we share in His everlasting glory.

Christ came not only to redeem us, but also to give us a clear picture of what God is like. Throughout the Old Testament, prophets had talked about God and intimate writings poured from the pens of those who knew God on a very personal basis. However, it took the Only Begotten to clarify forever the gentleness of God. Jesus did this well and the gentleness He exhibited still spills on the world.

One of the most poignant portraits of God was offered by Isaiah seven hundred years before Christ. In chapter 40, Isaiah seems to be standing on a mountain of holy prophecy peering through centuries to the time of the coming King. Much is said of the majesty of God, about His strength and overwhelming power. Then, hollowed in this hallowed chapter are words whose brushstrokes paint the portrait of God, "He shall feed his flock like a shepherd: he shall gather the lambs with his arm, and carry them in his bosom, and shall gently lead those that are with young" (Isa. 40:11).

David, who passionately sought for God's heart, left chiseled into time the picture of a gentle God. In a prayer of praise for the good and full life he led, David shouts, "For by thee I had run through a troop; by my God have I leaped over a wall" (2 Sam. 22:30). Then, he moves on to give the key to whatever success in life he had achieved,

"Thou hast also given me the shield of thy salvation; and thy *gentleness* hath made me great" (v. 36).

There was a time in David's life when he had bitterly failed and by all human standards should have been impeached and cast forever from the presence of God. Yet, in that moment God forgave and restored. It is true, punishment followed as it must, but David could certainly testify God had been gentle to him in his horrible but human failure. It must have been from this spirit he wrote in his most famous psalm, ". . . thy rod and thy staff they comfort me" (Ps. 23:4). The rod was used to beat off wild animals attacking the sheep, but the staff was for a far different purpose. At the end of the long staff there was a crook just large enough to fit snugly around the sheep's breast. When a sheep would fall off the path into one of the deep gullies the shepherd would not leave him there, but would reach down with the staff and lift him. David felt this lifting in his sin, a gentle but firm return to the path. No wonder David could sing, "Thy *gentleness* hath made me great."

Show Your Sentiment

G. K. Chesterton once said, "The meanest fear is the fear of sentimentality." So often we hide our sentiment and gentleness because we are afraid of being called "soft" or "weak." We need be reminded of Ralph W. Sockman's wise words, "Gentleness is a Divine trait; nothing is so strong as gentleness, and nothing is so gentle as real strength." These men are only echoing what prophets and preachers have long been saying. God's Word admonishes us to be gentle.

Some words that men write seem to ring with truth they have learned from bitter experience. I think so often of Paul and his last words to a young man he loved very deeply in the faith. Paul hoped Timothy would rise even higher than himself and avoid all the pitfalls he had experienced. In this mood he pours out his heart, "And the servant of the Lord must not strive; but must be *gentle* unto all men . . ." (2 Tim. 2:24). Then, to another son in the faith he writes, "Put them in mind . . . to speak evil of no man, to be no brawlers, but *gentle*, showing all meekness unto all men" (Titus 3:1, 2). These were not easy words for Paul to write because he by nature was not a gentle man. His mind, when penning these words, was no doubt thrust back to a day he wished he could forget.

Paul and Barnabas had worked together for many months. Paul owed Barnabas much because it was this trusting man who persuaded Christian leaders to give Paul a chance. Then an unfortunate incident parted them forever. The story is familiar: Paul insisted that young John Mark not accompany them again because of the first failure. Uncle Barnabas would have no part of this argument and stood firm. The Bible says, "And the contention was so sharp between them, that they departed asunder one from the other" (Acts 15:39). Perhaps if Paul would have been more bending, perhaps if he would have been more gentle, there never would have come this break between two godly men. Certainly, Paul was sorry, since later he asked Mark to join him in Rome, "for he is profitable to me for the ministry" (2 Tim. 4:11). Paul probably was plagued all his life about that time when he found to his horror he was most capable of acting quite contrary to Christian principle. From then on we find his epistles charged through with admonitions to be gentle. Paul must have suffered many tears over this angry moment in his life.

Other church leaders caught the fire of Paul's admonition, and James writes to young Christians, "But the wisdom that is from above is first pure, then peaceable, *gentle*, and easy to be intreated, full of mercy and good fruits, without partiality, and without hypocrisy" (James 3:17).

It is easy to be hard, strict, and legal. This provides a veneer of righteousness that men cannot see through and somehow we think they think us holy. We only fool ourselves, as they, like the African native, really feel that we are heartless and most un-Christlike. What a wonderful thing if we could say with Paul, "But we were gentle among you, even as a nurse cherisheth her children" (1 Thess. 2:7).

Some Christians heed admonitions to gentleness and treat those about them with great kindness, but are unmercifully hard on themselves. They exercise little understanding where their own faults are concerned. True, we should, like Paul, feel we are least of all the saints, but we cannot let this feeling of unworthiness keep us from effective service for the Master. Some have never forgiven themselves for past mistakes or great sins. Their lives are lived in torment, and beneath the surface is a soul writhing in agony. Tom Anderson was such a man.

For years Tom was tormented by the memory of his part in a fraternity escapade resulting in the death of one of his friends. Dogged by this he floundered from one job to another and finally separated from his wife. His life was a complete failure and he said, "The thought of my guilt would stop me in the middle of a handshake or a smile. It put a barrier between my wife and me."

Later, the news of Tom Anderson changed and he gained his old job back; his wife came back and he became successful and happy. Explaining what had happened Tom said, "I had an unexpected visit from the person I dreaded most to see—the mother of the college classmate who died.

"'Years ago,' she said, 'I found it in my heart, through prayer, to forgive you. Betty forgave you. So did your friends and employers. God forgave you.' Then she paused and said, 'You are the only person who hasn't forgiven, Tom Anderson. Who do you think you are to stand out against the people of this town and the Lord Almighty?'"

Tom told a friend, "I looked into her eyes and found there a kind of permission to be the person I might have been if her boy had lived. For the first time in my adult life I felt worthy to love and to be loved."

It is not only necessary to be forgiving and understanding of others, but we must also be so with ourselves. The destructive power of an unforgiving spirit toward oneself is overwhelming. Peter did not quit because he cursed; nor Thomas because he doubted; nor Mark because he ran away. They were gentle with themselves, and found the creative power of self-acceptance and self-forgiveness.

Growing into Gentleness

Like any other fruit of the Spirit, this one too must grow. A man does not just decide to be gentle. This is a work of the Spirit in his life and the more mature spiritually we become, the more gentle we are. However, there are some active things we can do to cultivate gentleness in our character.

Take time for tenderness. There is a tragic story about Lenin that persists to this day, revealing much about his inner soul. Vladimir Ulyanov was born in 1870 to a family that would suffer many tragedies in the years to come. Later, he used the pen name, Lenin, to promote his revolutionary ideas. He wrapped himself in his revolutionary work until he lost almost all capacity for human tenderness. Those about him said he was a most miserable man.

Although married, Lenin gave little love to his wife Krupskaya. One night she rose exhausted from her vigil beside her dying mother and asked Lenin, who was writing at a table, to awaken her if her mother needed her. Lenin agreed and Krupskaya collapsed into bed. The next morning she awoke to find her mother dead and Lenin still at work. Distraught, she confronted Lenin, who replied, "You told me to wake you if your mother needed you. She died. She didn't need you."

It is possible to wrap oneself in a cause, a job, a hobby, a sport, until there is no time or attempt for tenderness.

71

And, often the cause is even a good one. Most of us remember singing the Civil War song, "John Brown's Body." However, few of us remember that while John Brown was driven by the saintly desire to free the slaves, his wife and thirteen children were back in the mountains starving. History records nine of his children actually died of malnutrition and two more were killed in his wild raids. Here was a man dedicated to a noble cause, but who would not take time to show tenderness to his own family. Few people can admire men like this.

Contrast these men with the life of our Lord. There has been no man before or since with such an important message or cause. Yet, we see Him taking time to be gentle to the small children crowding about Him. He visits with a woman at the well and sparks a fire in her heart that burns with joy. He stoops in the sand, lowering Himself in the eyes of the religionist to help a fallen woman redeem her battered pride and restore some dignity to a sorry soul. It is heart-warming to think of how much time Jesus spent just being tender and gentle with people. Sentiment cannot live in an atmosphere of clock-watching. Time must be taken for tenderness. Great people not only have heart for tenderness, but also make time. Ernie Pyle, the beloved war correspondent, was never too busy or too harried with deadlines to sit down and listen to the woes of a soldier or to write letters home for wounded boys.

Eliminate the shadow wars. One thing that destroys our gentleness and calmness of spirit is the imaginary wars we wage in our minds. We muse over tense situations with neighbors, friends or mates and pledge, "I'm really going to tell them." By giving in to this temptation our imaginary war suddenly becomes very real and we lose all hope for gentleness and we "do unto others before they have a chance to do unto us." The classic story of the "jack" best illustrates these shadow wars.

A fellow was speeding down a country road late one night when his tire blew out. When he opened his trunk he discovered he had forgotten to replace the jack the last time he had used it. He looked around and saw a light in the distance and began walking toward it with the thought he could borrow a jack at the farmhouse.

Musing to himself he opened his imaginary conversation with, "I'll just knock on the door and say I'm in trouble and would he please lend me a jack. He'll say sure, help yourself." Walking and thinking further the man noticed the light in the house had gone out. He thought, "Now he's gone to bed and he'll be mad because I'll have to wake him so I better offer him a dollar." Walking on he now mused, "What if he is away and his wife is alone and she will be afraid to open the door. Maybe I had better offer five dollars."

By this time the poor fellow had worked himself up so much he said out loud, "Five dollars! All right, but not a cent more. What are you trying to do, rob a man?" This brought him to the house and he knocked loudly. When the farmer leaned out the window and asked, "Who's there?" the angry stranger yelled, "You and your stupid jack! You can keep the wretched thing!"

So many things we face are imaginary and if we learned to keep our mind stayed on Christ we would find perfect peace. And, from this peace would spring the gentleness of spirit which is the fruit of the Spirit. Jesus warned against creating imaginary situations and making plans on what to say when He noted, "But when they shall lead you, and deliver you up, take no thought beforehand what ye shall speak, neither do ye premeditate: but whatsoever shall be given you in that hour, that speak ye: for it is not ye that speak, but the Holy Ghost" (Mark 13:11).

Be gentle at all times. Somewhere as a child I heard the amusing story of a deacon who decided to get off the "gospel train" just long enough to "whip" a brother who had done him wrong. The story goes that when he wanted to get back on, the train had already left the station. I

73

don't know the truth of this humorous tale, but it does encourage us to be true at all times.

There are certain times when it is difficult to be gentle. When nerves are ragged and tensions stab us with sharp and biting pains it is hard to be kind. Yet, in these times we are to exercise gentleness. Paul carried in his body many wounds of suffering. No doubt he was never free of pain and yet in all this he was gentle. In times of illness we need keep a double watch on ourselves that gentleness will not be pushed out by pain.

When one rises to new authority there is also temptation to lose one's gentleness. Nero was known for his kindness before he became the ruler of Rome, but after he assumed the role, tyranny became his trademark. He drove wildly through Roman streets running over those who got in his way, while the tarred and burning bodies of saints lit his garden at night. The test of genuine gentleness comes when we suddenly are thrust to a time of power and strength. I think so often of Abe Lincoln who refused to heed the hounds who yelped for him to crush the South. In his full executive power he simply stood his ground, demanding "malice toward none and charity for all."

True, it is farther to Calvary for some than others. Some people seem to be born with a tender nature. However, if Christ-likeness is reached there must be the crucifying of self and the drive toward gentleness. How often we need simply to brood in God's presence and think deeply of the personality of our Savior, until that tenderness spills over into our lives. The late Powell Davies of Washington, D. C., wrote, "We are all lonely under the stars, all strangers and sojourners here on earth." If we could learn the urgency of the need of gentleness then we would be challenged to let the Spirit that dwelled in Christ become the guide of our lives.

Try the Tender Touch

In our age of guided missiles and misguided men there is desperate need for us to learn how to share gentleness.

It seems strange that in an age when we can reach the moon, bounce signals off far planets, and receive pictures from whirling satellites we have great difficulty communicating tenderness to those about us. Dr. Smiley Blanton suggests we start by learning again the value of the tender touch.

This eminent physician talks about the healing power of simply touching someone you love. An invisible virtue seems to leave one body and transfer itself to the other by touch. Dr. Blanton suggests walking with your arm around your wife or holding hands around the dinner table when you say grace.

A few years ago I learned the importance of touch. After being called to a church where small tensions had torn some people asunder I tried to heal the breach by sermons about unity. After months of trying, the tension still remained and bickering persisted. Then, one night I merely asked the people to come to the front of the church. Then, I requested the men put their arms around other men and the women around other women and tell them they loved them. Halfway embarrassed, they did this as a favor to their pastor, and some certainly did not have their heart in it. One elderly man grumbled as he reluctantly obeyed, "There are other ways to show love than by this silly trick."

Nevertheless it worked. The simple touching of one another and communicating of love began to heal wounds that had been festering too long. Years later my heart would be thrilled to see and feel the deep love between members of that congregation. I would not recommend this procedure as a panacea for all problems, but there is something healing in the tender touch.

A distinguished judge said he had seen hundreds of juvenile offenders and their parents brought before his court. Yet, never once in all those years had he seen a parent touch a youngster, or put his arm around his shoulder, or show any physical sign of affection. Contrast this with the father of the prodigal son who fell on his son's neck and kissed him.

Jesus used touch to communicate. He laid hands on the sick, washed the disciples' feet, and cuddled little children. Babylonians centuries before had used touch as part of their healing art. In her memoirs Concert Pianist Marta Korwin tells of her volunteer work as a nurse during World War II. "Late at night," she wrote, "going through the wards, I noticed a soldier whose face was buried in a pillow. He was sobbing and moaning into the pillow so that he would disturb no one.

"I looked at my hands and felt that I might be able to help him. If I could transmit vibrations in harmony through the piano, why could I not transmit harmony directly, without an instrument? When I took the boy's head in my hands, he grabbed them with such force that I thought his nails would be embedded in my flesh. I prayed that the harmony of the world could come to help me alleviate the pain. His sobs quieted down, and then his hands released their grip and he was asleep." This is the power of the tender touch.

There is so much hardness in the world that I am convinced the greatest evangelistic thrust of our time will come in a revival of gentleness. People respond to love. There would still be need for hell-fire preaching, but hungry, lost, lonely, heartbroken souls are seeking for a Savior, and so many need guidance—not pronouncement of doom. Gentle leading would help them find Christ, the panacea for all problems. Most people are running scared, and somehow if they knew God loves and cares and that His people love and care what happens to them, they would forget many foolish fears and learn to live.

In a frustrating world where many are floundering, there needs to be someone who reminds people that Jesus said, "For God sent not his Son into the world to condemn the world; but that the world through him might be saved" (John 3:17). Be gentle, for everyone you meet is fighting a battle. True nobility comes from a gentle heart.

7

The Different Drummer

George Clark's cartoons more than often reveal human nature for what it is. In one sketch he shows two rather large ladies talking over tea about their association with faddish diet fraternities. One said, "My reducing club is a great success. We've lost 148 pounds. However, none of it is mine personally."

In this fraternity of humanity we often like to talk of those great individuals who stand out for their unadulterated goodness. We weep when the world loses a Tom Dooley or Albert Schweitzer. We swell to great emotion upon hearing names like David Livingston or Paul Carlson. Tragically, too often little of this special kind of goodness they possessed is personally ours.

There is a certain breed of men who do not seek fame or fortune and often try to avoid it, but they cannot. They gain the world's imagination and affection because they seek different goals and have higher convictions. They have a goodness that although hard to explain is very evident. Henry David Thoreau spent long hours thinking about such men.

Thoreau, that rugged New England individualist of the last century, was once jailed because he refused to pay a poll tax to a state that supported slavery. Soon his close friend, Ralph Waldo Emerson, came to visit him, peered through the bars, and anxiously asked, "Why, Henry, what are you doing in there?"

"Nay, Ralph," Thoreau pointedly replied, "The question is, What are you doing out there?"

From this and similar experiences Thoreau defended his position and those of other such men when he wrote, "If a man does not keep pace with his companions perhaps it is because he hears a different drummer. Let him step to the music he hears, however measured or far away."

Critics said of Woodrow Wilson, "He talks like Jesus Christ." No greater compliment could be given any man, but it was not meant as a compliment. However, Wilson listened to a different drummer and his great goodness outlasted the sneers of the skeptics.

Some time ago I spoke to thirty young people who were preparing to make decisions about their occupations. First, I asked what they desired to do in life and then Why? Their answers reflected the feelings of our age and not one was without selfish motive. Most often their decisions were based on how much money they could make or how much attention they would receive.

Then I asked them to list the men they felt are the really great personalties of history. As expected they listed names of men known for their self-sacrifice and service. My heart was heavy because while these young people realized true greatness is goodness, not one wanted to make the personal sacrifice to achieve such for himself.

Perhaps I am being a little hard on those young people. Perhaps before they made their final decisions for life they recognized the truth Jesus set forth when he said that to find one's life he must lose it. However, it does point up the fact too many people lack personal goodness and one questions why more do not possess the courage for greatness. The answer, of course, is that achieving goodness involves struggle against almost overwhelming odds and too many feel the fight not worth it.

Grappling for Goodness

A young man wrote an eminent clergyman and announced he was giving up religion and simply would live by the golden rule. The basis for his decision lay in the fact that in college he was made to see all the evil of the world and wondered how a good God could permit such heartache.

The minister wisely replied, "You are a young man, and I am now in my 80s. You write about living the good life as though you could blow on your hands and do it. That has not been my experience. Right living is a challenging affair! It involves a constant and sometimes devastating struggle against temptation. It costs self-discipline, self-sacrifice, self-control, courage to refuse conformity and to stand up against popular wrongs."

Winding up his remarkable answer, the preacher wrote, "I have seen many magnificent comebacks from moral abysses—alcoholism, vice, criminality, or what you will—but I never saw one that did not involve a recovery of faith in God." The simple fact is living in pure goodness is not easy. True goodness requires spiritual stamina that exceeds just a determination to be just.

George Washington Carver was a man who had this special goodness. Born a slave, Carver struggled against tremendous odds to achieve an education. Finally, after years of abuse he finished his master's degree and was asked to accept a position with Iowa University. It was a coveted job and no other Negro had ever had such a high place. At last he could relax and enjoy the comforts of his society. People at the university loved him and sat eagerly in his classes.

Then a letter came from Booker T. Washington asking the young scientist to join him in a dream to educate Negroes of the South. Leaving his comfortable position,

Carver traveled to the parched cottonlands of the South to live and work among his starving people. Years of sacrifice and insult followed, but slowly and surely this great soul saved his people from sure starvation and brought them a dignity that would raise them forever from the slave class.

When questioned about his brilliance, Carver always said the good Lord gave him everything. He refused to accept money for any of his discoveries, rather choosing to give them free to anyone who asked for them. Three presidents claimed him as a friend. Great industries vied for his service and even Thomas Edison offered him a beautiful new laboratory and a $100,000 a year salary. When Carver turned it down critics commented, "If you had all this money you could help your people." Carver simply replied, "If I had all that money I might forget my people." The epitaph on his tomb bares the sacred soul of this great man, "He could have added fame and fortune, but cared for neither, he found happiness and honor in being helpful to the world." This type of goodness always costs greatly.

The Divided Heart

Each man has found he has potential for great goodness or great evil. Robert Louis Stevenson's story of good Dr. Jekyll and bad beast Hyde brilliantly shows potential for both. And, just when we think we rise to great goodness, then evil bares its ugly teeth in our souls and we seem to fall back. However, it should be remembered that all men, even those great ones mentioned before, had the same division of heart. Somehow they learn to choke out the evil and cultivate good. This brings us to Paul's statement, "The fruit of the Spirit is goodness."

Division of heart was recognized long before Stevenson thought up his clever story or Freud began piercing the veneer of human personality. David cried out long ago, "Teach me thy ways, O Lord; I will walk in thy truth: *unite* my heart to fear thy name" (Ps. 86:11).

David prays his heart will be united *to fear God*. Unfortunately, a heart can be united to despise good and commit great evil. This we saw in Nazi Germany. Millions of words have and will be poured out about those unspeakable horrors when the greatest realization of man's tremendous capacity for evil bared itself.

Our hearts still shudder when we read of those thousands of fathers who knelt naked beside graves they had dug, holding their hands over the eyes of their sons as German pistols exploded in the backs of their heads. We cringe when we think of the Nazi scientific experiments of injecting children with TB germs and watching them die. Genocide was so shocking it is even today hard to hear the horror of five million dead. The utter and absolute depravity of man and his horrible capacity for evil became most apparent. And, Nazis are not the only ones to blame. All of us have seen men and women who are apparently dedicated to evil, with hearts united to hate God and goodness.

From the realization of how evil humanity can be we cry for God to make us good. From such a desire we can find true goodness. John Bunyan, speaking of *Christian's* journey to the City of God, says a desire will carry a man to God if 10,000 oppose it; "without the desire all is rain upon stones."

Centuries after David, the apostle James would deal with the divided heart in more harsh terms, "Out of the same mouth proceedeth blessing and cursing. My brethren, these things ought not so to be. Doth a fountain send forth at the same place sweet water and bitter? Can the fig tree, my brethren, bear olive berries? either a vine, figs? so can no fountain both yield salt water and fresh" (James 3:10-13). He went on to say that real wisdom is complete purity and goodness.

So far we have been talking of great goodness and great evil. However, it should be remembered the ultimate in

81

either is sown first in seeds of everyday goodness or evil. Our great acts are but extensions of our small ones and the habits we sow in the springtime of our life we reap in the autumn. These men did not suddenly become filled with great goodness or great evil. Rather, it was in the warp and woof of their character and they crushed out one and cultivated the other. Therefore, it is absolutely necessary to bring our discussion to the lowest levels of our lives and deal with goodness in the mundane things.

It is easy to say we would react with goodness when some boldly attack all that which is sacred. However, unless we have buttressed ourselves within with goodness we will not stand in the blast of bold attack. Goodness is born of God's Spirit, the ultimate source of all goodness, and takes full sway of our lives only as we give control to Him.

In recent years relativism has gained a stronger foothold. It is an argument old as man, but today theologians are talking about "situational ethics," or "circumstantialism." You might hear the terms, "occasionalism," "contextualism," or "actualism." These words describe the old theory that says all things are relative. Rather than observe a set of rules one must wait for the situation to present itself and then decide what is moral or good.

Arguments have been presented by both sides of the issue. While the war of words wages we laypersons still must make decisions determining our destiny, about what is the moral or good thing to do. We deserve some straight answers to this problem. Therefore, regardless of the outcome of present arguments, there are some simple steps we can take to assure we are stamping out evil and cultivating good.

Whom Do We Trust?

Paul observed the law was given so we might know when we have done that which is not good for ourselves, society, and God. The foundation fact says there must be a basis for judgment or each man is a law unto himself. The dangerous problem with situational ethics is what Israel experienced during the judges, "But every man did that which was right in his own eyes" (Judg. 17:6). However, it was noted earlier, "The children of Israel did evil in the eyes of the Lord" (2:11). Here we have the staggering thought that while something may seem right in our own eyes it is contrary to what God desires.

In the arrogance of youth I entered college knowing far more, I felt, than those older. I shall never forget the first day of my psychology class when the wise professor placed a series of thirty-two questions on the board and asked for our answers. They were simple questions and "common sense" would give you the answers. There were questions like, "Do people of superior intelligence have higher insanity and suicide rates than the general population?" Boldly I put "yes." Another question, "Children have a greater capacity for learning than adults, which makes the childhood the 'golden age' for learning." Again I blatantly wrote "True" and thought, "College is a snap." However, to my horror I found when the test was graded I had not only missed these two questions, but sixteen more. The professor said to the class, "The first rule of psychology is never trust your common sense." He drove us to our books seeking for these answers and we realized immediately how much we had to learn.

Thousands of years ago God had warned against arrogance and self-trust when He inspired the proverbist to write, "There is a way which seemeth right unto a man, but the end thereof are the ways of death" (14:12). Situational ethics can be most precarious because, as Jeremiah observed, "The heart is deceitful above all things, and desperately wicked: who can know it?" (Jer. 17:9). All of which drives us to the penetrating question, "Whom or what do we trust to give us basis for truth?"

The crowd is wrong. The teenage argument, "Everybody is doing it," is just as shabby as it sounds. Our morality cannot be as unstable as fads and fashions of the masses. A few centuries ago the crowd knew tomatoes would poison and even warned against taking baths for health reasons. They told Edison his light bulb would never work and the cotton gin was scorned while in the experimental stages. The crowd is often wrong and the argument so elementary we need explore it no further.

However, taking a stand against the crowd is not easy. This is a struggle that exposes our strength or weakness. In South Africa, where the climate is one of racism and where black men often suffer humiliation by white inhabitants, a Bantu was sent to the theater to get tickets for his white employer. There was a single line and upon inquiry he was told to get in the white man's line although in South Africa this is forbidden.

Suddenly a black-haired youth elbowed him out of line. This haughty action was followed by similar actions of a teenage girl. Then a real bull of a man with closely cropped hair seized the native and hurled him into the street. The theater manager told him to get back in line, but again he was thrown out.

Then a voice sounded clear above the rumble of the complaints. A man of about fifty, with whitened temples and in the open neck attire of a farmer, shouted with a voice ringing with threat and authority, "Let this fellow in. What's the matter with you?" The crowd cowered and the lowly native was placed in front. The South African farmer risked his reputation and the crowd's disapproval, but he stood firm. This is goodness. And, it costs.

Contrast this with a group of Indiana teenagers recently arrested for shoplifting. They admitted they did not need the merchandise, but stole it because everybody was doing it. Investigation revealed they did not feel they had done wrong since the crowd had placed a sanction on it. Masses cannot determine morality. Sometimes we stand alone and if we crush goodness we risk our very lives. But, to be a leader we must be in front. Sadly, the commentary of our age is that of T. S. Eliot, ". . . the hollow men . . . the stuffed men leaning together head-piece filled with straw. Alas."

Follow your feelings. Another problem with situational ethics is the admonition to follow your feelings. However, following feelings is as fickle as following masses.

A giant jet fell like a dying sparrow. It was too late for the pilot to parachute, so the mass of metal crushed its victim as it plunged deeply into the plowed field.

Sirens screamed. Women wept. Men worked futilely around the twisted wreckage. Officials began piecing the story of the crash together and told anxious reporters that the probable cause was vertigo.

Later, an Air Force flying officer explained in simple terms what vertigo means. He said at times the atmospheric conditions tend to confuse pilots. They lose all sense of direction and perspective. They may even feel they are flying upside down although the instruments indicate all is well. He said the greatest temptation during this time is to take controls in one's own hands and try to right the plane. This mistake is often fatal and probably was that which caused the crash of the Air Force jet.

We have all seen tragic individuals who have tried to take the controls of their lives in their own hands and live by their feelings. It is sort of a spiritual vertigo that often leads to tragedy. The way that seems right ends in despair and the world has witnessed the heartbreaking end of this despair in tragic lives like those of Marilyn Monroe, Lord Byron, and Diana Barrymore.

Find wiser men and wiser words. Some people pin their morality on intellectuals of this world. The philosophers become guides for our society and we feel those with higher education and intellectual capacity are more qualified than we to rule on morality.

More than half of Hitler's high command were highly educated men. Most had their master's degree and several their doctorates. Certainly we could not say they were sane judges of what was good for themselves and society. Sometimes, even the more educated are biased. In that psychology test mentioned previously, one of the true-false questions was, "When a person learns, he always improves." Our professor pointed out, "Learning is popularly considered in terms of improvement. But while learning can accomplish such desirable changes it can also produce opposite effects." Studies of the morals of some of the most learned men testify to this truth.

Some time ago a most shocking and yet thrilling story came out of the South. A rough mountaineer gave his heart to Christ and began the battle of controlling his fiery temper and foul tongue. He did exceptionally well, but then came to his pastor with a confession.

"Pastor," he said, "I haven't had a single fight or cussed once since I became a Christian. But, I just came from a very narrow escape and if I'm wrong I want you and God to forgive me.

"Here is what happened," he said. "Yesterday I went to the doctor's office to have a little patchup done. Just when I started to go in for my turn they brought a little Negro boy in who had been hit by a car. One arm was badly broken and the bone protruded from the skin. The doctor glanced at him and then turned to me and said, 'Come in and I'll fix you up!'

"'No,' I replied, 'Fix this boy up first. He needs help and I can wait.' The doctor said, 'No, he can wait.' I said, 'No, I can wait.' Then the doctor said, 'Do you think I'm going to keep a white man waiting while I fix up some nigger kid?'

"Pastor," the husky farmer went on, "Maybe my answer was wrong, but I said, 'You will fix this boy now or I'll beat the hell out of you.'"

Certainly the farmer's language could have been improved, but his deed certainly could not have. The tragic truth of this story is that education did not improve the doctor's prejudice, but an uneducated swain was wiser in goodness and love. It is crystal clear that goodness does not improve with education. Education might make man more skillful and less rude, but still the heart is haughty and hateful.

Trite but True

Preachers have said it so long that the truth almost becomes trite. However, the eternal fact is that the only basis for goodness is God's Word. In an age of relativism and denial of past mores it is important to realize that without a foundation the framework of goodness cannot be built. Therefore, Paul says the fruit of the Spirit is goodness—establishing forever its source and sustenance. David said he hid God's Word in his heart that he might not sin against God. All of Psalm 119 is charged through with praise for this foundation which gives light, life, guidance, and truth. Ignoring this foundation ushers us to relativism and its fallacies which one can readily observe.

In the past decade many of the institutions and traditions of man have come under severe scrutiny. This is not always bad, but there is a temptation to throw these out without knowing their value and understanding the necessity for them. It would be well to remember they have survived because they are useful for the overall survival of man. In recent years the Christian funeral came under such attack.

In several cleverly written books much was discussed about the American way of death. Reforms were suggested, and with haste most of us were willing to shed ourselves completely of the whole funeral idea. However, wiser men went into extensive research and discovered the tremendous therapeutic value of the funeral service as the easiest and best method of withdrawing love from the deceased to reinvest it into another person or cause. Several searching books have been written now, crying for a new look at this time honored institution. Dr. Edgar N. Jackson says, "At a time when practically all the competent and objective research is going in one direction, the recommendations in regard to reforms in the funeral practice appear to discount or ignore these findings and go their separate way with a heavy charge of emotion and a breakdown of objectivity."

What is true of this one institution is certainly true of the entire spectrum. Today psychiatrists and psychologists are standing beside the preacher in an attempt to show the value and practicality of the time-honored wisdom of Scripture. Yet, we seem to plunge headlong, ignoring this foundation of truth. But without this foundation we vacillate between right and wrong until relativism ruins us.

Ezekiel seemed to understand this generation when he talked of a conspiracy of God's prophets, who went about as roaring lions, ravening the prey, devouring souls, profaning that which is sacred, and seeing no difference between the holy and the profane things. He concludes his passioned plea with, "And I sought for a man among them that should make up the hedge, and stand in the gap before me for the land that I should not destroy it. But I found none" (Ezek. 22:30).

Whatever goodness we will know in these years or in the times to come will come only from the source of all goodness, God. Goodness is a fruit of the Spirit, and though it might cost dearly, it is necessary for our survival. We cannot live through another Nazi regime. With the potential for nuclear annihilation haunting us, the seeds of hate must be crushed before they burst forth in full fury. The most towering issue of our time is world survival, but we can survive only if we crush the evil in our lives and cultivate the fruit of goodness. We must say with Giovanni Papini, "Jesus had just one aim, to transform men from beasts into human beings by means of love, to save us from animality by a force more powerful than force."

8

While the Church Sleeps

When Orville and Wilbur Wright finally succeeded in keeping their homemade airplane in the air for fifty-nine seconds on December 17, 1903, they rushed a telegram to their sister in Dayton, Ohio, telling of this great accomplishment.

The telegram read, "First sustained flight today fifty-nine seconds. Hope to be home by Christmas." Upon receiving the news the sister was so excited about the success that she rushed to the newspaper office and gave the telegram to the editor. The next morning—believe it or not—the newspaper headline stated in black, bold letters, "Popular Local Bicycle Merchants To Be Home For Holidays."

The scoop of the century was missed because an editor missed the point. We laugh when we read this account but many times we have missed the point of some Scriptures because we have read them too casually and not let their deep meaning sink into our souls. This is especially true of faith as the fruit of the Spirit.

Careful consideration of the original text indicates the word *faith* would more correctly be translated "faithfulness." Faith in its general sense indicates our basis for

89

belief and therefore is the root not the fruit. Faithfulness more clearly defines what Paul had in mind when he said the outgrowth of a Spirit-filled life is faith.

Multiple testimony in Scripture indicates the virtue of faithfulness. The proverbist said, "A faithful man shall abound with blessings" (28:20). Paul writes to Corinth, "Moreover it is required in stewards, that a man be found faithful" (1 Cor. 4:2). Then Jesus says through John, "Be thou faithful unto death, and I will give thee a crown of life" (Rev. 2:10).

In our age of pleasure-seeking and selfish pursuit it is imperative the man of God be faithful in his high calling of building the Kingdom. We have been ushered into an age of apathy when the church sleeps while men die and those dying are so sedated by Satan they do not ever realize their danger. In this age the watchman must be awake and faithful to his calling.

Age of Apathy

A giant claw reached out from a submerged iceberg and ripped a 300-foot gash in the side of the unsinkable *Titanic*, plunging it to the bottom of the sea. On that horror-filled night of April 15, 1912, laughter turned to screaming, merriment to weeping, as 1,517 souls were swallowed by the black and icy waters. The most tragic truth was that most, if not all, could have been saved. The *Titanic* sank within sight of another ship!

Subsequent testimony revealed officers of the *Californian* watched while the *Titanic* was swallowed by the icy sea. They testified they did not realize what was happening although distress rockets filled the sky for over an hour. Testimony of those recounting the tragedy revealed the *Titanic* sailed within sight of the *Californian* at 11:30 P.M. and radio contact was made. The *Californian* was bedded down for the night when at 11:00 P.M. the captain and wireless operator went to bed. Ten minutes later the *Titanic* slammed into the razorsharp iceberg.

Aboard the *Titanic*, now sinking, officers tried to re-establish radio contact. After failing, because of the sleeping captain and wireless operator, distress rockets were sent up. The *Californian* officer on duty called down the speaking tube to the sleeping captain notifying him of the signals. The captain asked, "Are they company signals?" Flares and Roman candles were used as company signals between passing ships at night. White rockets meant distress. The novice officer said, "I don't know." The captain went back to sleep.

Shortly before 2:00 A.M. the *Titanic* made a last desperate effort by sending eight giant rockets arching in the sky. This time the young officer delivered the message in person, awakening the *Californian's* captain. Recorded testimony reveals he asked, "Were they white?" The anxious sailor said, "All white." "What time is it?" the captain asked. "Two-oh-five" was the answer. The captain made no further reply but rolled over and went back to sleep.

Fifteen minutes later there were no more rockets or light. The *Titanic* had been sucked to the bottom of the sea, a watery coffin for 1500 souls. The investigating committee's report concluded, "The night was clear. The sea was smooth. When she first saw the rockets the *Californian* could have pushed through the ice without any serious risk and so have come to the aid of the *Titanic*. Had she done so she might have saved many, if not all, of the lives that were lost."

If we believe the Bible we must realize we are engaged in a violent struggle for the souls of men. It is more than just convincing a man he should go to our church. There is eternal destiny at stake and Jesus said the only entrance into eternal life is belief in God's plan of salvation. But, it seems some in the church sleep while many die without hearing of Christ who can save them. The apostles warned of deaf ears, hardened hearts, and blinded eyes. The tragic thing is that often while the church sleeps, souls perish. Often they sink within our sight.

91

One of the most disturbing chapters in the Bible concerns a vision Ezekiel had. Recorded in chapter 9 of his brilliant book, the prophet sees six men called before God, each with a destructive weapon in his hand. One man among them is clothed in linen with a writer's ink-horn by his side. God says to him, "Go through the midst of the city, through the midst of Jerusalem, and set a mark upon the foreheads of the men that sigh and cry for all the abominations that be done in the midst thereof." Turning to the others God speaks, "Go ye after him through the city, and smite: let not your eye spare, neither have ye pity; slay utterly young and old, both maids and little children: but come not near any man upon whom is the mark."

The footnote God adds is a frightening one, "And begin at my sanctuary." The vision is clear and the application simple. God was concerned because no one seemed to care that corruption had swallowed goodness. In another place the prophet quotes God, "And I sought for a man among them that should make up the hedge, and stand in the gap before me for the land, that I should not destroy it: but I found none. Therefore have I poured out mine indignation upon them; I have consumed them with the fire of my wrath: their own way have I recompensed upon their head, saith the Lord God" (Ezek. 22:30, 31).

While it is wonderful to speak of the great goodness of God, still part of the message of the Gospel is impending judgment for the unbeliever. The angel told the apostles, "Go, stand and speak in the temple to the people *all* the words of this life" (Acts 5:20). Therefore, words of warning are in order and the Spirit-filled believer will be faithful in discharging his or her responsibility.

It is not always easy or pleasant to take seriously the task of warning and witnessing. However, it is imperative that we do so. Not all heed and certainly not all will believe. Most usually, people do not even realize the precarious predicament they are in if they are without

Christ. Similar ignorance was evident on the *Titanic* that night in 1912.

Testimony given to the subcommittee of the United States Senate's Committee on Commerce and the British Board of Trade showed the *Titanic's* crew ignored warning after warning. They sped on through the night although they had been told a great ice field was ahead. Just minutes after turning a warning away the *Titanic* plunged into the submerged iceberg.

The last warning received was from a nearby ship which had seen previous warnings ignored. The *Titanic* arrogantly responded, "Shut up. Shut up. I am talking to Cape Race. You are jamming my signals."

Testimony revealed the *Titanic* was talking to Cape Race, the relay point, about such things as turning down the sheets in the millionaire's homes, arranging for chauffeurs to meet them at the docks, what to prepare for the first meal home, and other domestic problems of those aboard this floating palace. They were too busy to heed warnings.

Jesus often spoke of those so busy making a living they forget to make a life. He told about a rich farmer who was so involved in building bigger barns he forgot to build for eternity. Tragically, this is so often the situation of modern man in our age of apathy. However, regardless of their reaction our responsibility is to issue the word of warning. Paul states the fruit of the Spirit is faithfulness.

Song for Our Century

Israel was chosen by God to deliver His message to the world and they became so involved with His blessings they forgot their responsibility. In fact when His Son came to consummate redemption's plan their arrogance forbade them to accept Him. Their sins were prophesied in the song Moses taught them just before his demise. It would be well for members of Christ's grafted in Israel to read and remember lest we too lose our perspective.

For forty years Moses had half-led and half-driven a nomadic nation toward a new homeland. Now he felt drawn to his "long home" and wished to pass on points to ponder in days ahead. Under the Holy Spirit's inspiration he penned the majestic words of a great hymn which still speaks with such force one can almost feel the powerful shadow of Moses falling across the pages (Deut. 32:1-43). This old, yet profound song is certainly applicable in our time.

Moses sets the pace for the psalm by saying God has designated Israel as His own portion. Moses makes certain the people realize the significance of this selection and makes much of the personal protection of a loving Father. However, God does not pamper a people without purpose. Jesus would later remind Israel, "Unto whom much is given, much also is required."

Israel prospered but problems arose in this prosperity. Moses says, "Jeshurun [the upright one] waxed fat and kicked." Preachers often say the greatest temptation to forget God is not in hard times but in good times. This is apparently what happened to Israel, for when they prospered they forgot God, the source of their special blessing.

For centuries the church has not suffered severe strife like that which tore at its throat the first three centuries following Christ. Pressure from the outside sought to crush the struggling church and false teachers within sowed seeds of discord. Still, the tiny church marched on to conquer with its creed. Some feel in our age of religious freedom the church has grown fat and lost its dynamics. This certainly is not true in all quarters, but God's portion, for the past two thousand years, the church, could be more effective than it now is. Perhaps we have grown fat.

Moses says Israel had taken five disastrous steps downward. It would be wise to reevaluate our position as "modern Israel" to see if there is temptation to follow in their folly.

94

They forsook God. Moses charges, ". . . then he forsook God which made him." Too often there is temptation to think we have "arrived" because of our personal dynamics, personality, or innate goodness. However, the psalmist states, "Know ye that the Lord he is God: it is he that hath made us, and not we ourselves" (Ps. 100:3). Add to this the words, "For promotion cometh neither from the east, nor from the west, nor from the south. But God is the judge: he putteth down one, and setteth up another" (Ps. 75:6, 7).

In moments when we are tempted to spiritual pride it would be wise to remind ourselves of our origins and sing, "To God be the glory, great things He hath done." Any success we have as a church or as individuals is only because He has blessed our efforts and given the increase. In other ranks a man might drive himself to the top. But, in the service of the Lord it is God who gives what we have and He is not only the source of our original strength, but also of our continuing strength. Jesus said it succinctly when He talked of the Vine and branches. As long as we remain in the Vine there is the life-giving and sustaining flow of His power and presence. Israel forgot this and tragedy resulted.

They took God lightly. Moses laments, ". . . [they] lightly esteemed the Rock of his salvation." Salvation for Israel had been miraculous. Beginning with preservation through Joseph, God led and later broke bonds of slavery through the plagues pronounced by Moses. Following this came dramatic deliverances in desert places. Moses eloquently records, "He found him in a desert land, and in the waste howling wilderness; he led him about, he instructed him, he kept him as the apple of his eye."

Then, Moses moves on to record the personal protection of Jehovah in the eloquent eagle allegory: "As an eagle stirreth up her nest, fluttereth over her young, spreadeth abroad her wings, taketh them, beareth them on her wings: So the Lord alone did lead him. . . ." The great leader goes on to tell of the success God affords His

95

people: "He made him to ride on the high places of the earth, that he might eat the increase of the fields." Salvation, protection, and success were all given, but still Israel did not appreciate Jehovah's fatherly hands, but lightly esteemed the Giver.

Much is said about God's great grace and love. Often there is a temptation to lightly esteem Him and feel, "He'll understand and say, 'Well done.'" However, Moses and all other great prophets had tremendous respect and reverence for God. He is the Eternal Creator and we can never reduce Him to our own personal God who serves us in our whims and pleasures. Too often some take too lightly His forgiveness and mercy, without remembering that although He is loving, He is also holy and just. Paul reminds us there is a day coming when we must give an account for the deeds we have done in the flesh.

They served strange gods. "They provoked him to anger with strange gods, with abominations provoked they him to anger." Even the Red Sea, manna, and miraculous clothing incidents did not keep Israel from confusing true worship with that of pagan peoples. They took strange gods and longed for the sensual worship of the pagan nations about them.

Sometimes we do not think this downfall typical of that in our century. Unfortunately, people still worship strange gods even though not overtly. There are those who bow to the gods of sports, position, money, entertainment—they unconsciously worship such things through their ambitions and attitudes. In our age there is much to tear one away from the true God. It might be said that anything that replaces God as the center of one's life is that which takes His place. Satan offers many diversions, but God alone must be worshiped. Tragic stories of those who have worshiped strange gods appear regularly. The suicide of sex symbols and the tragic demise of the successful in business and politics portray the emptiness of offering one's life and substance to strange gods who satisfy only the sensual.

They sacrificed unto demons. Moses accuses, "They sacrificed unto devils, not to God." This referred to the gods of Canaan, since demonism is the dynamic of idolatry. Paul mentions this sacrifice to demons again in 1 Corinthians 10. The word *sacrifice* indicates giving to someone else what one would rather keep.

In our century there is abundant sacrifice to the strange gods already mentioned. We seem to have the money to spend for that which satisfies the sensual; yet the church of God is encumbered with debts. Paul mentions "Owe no man anything, but to love one another . . ." (Rom. 13:8). Can it be that in our secular society we are sacrificing to devils as Israel did and robbing God of *His* tithes and *our* offerings? Haggai clearly tells later Israelites, "Ye have sown much, and bring in little; ye eat, but ye have not enough; ye drink, but ye are not filled with drink; ye clothe you, but there is none warmed; and he that earneth wages earneth wages to put it into a bag with holes" (1:6). Explaining why this has occurred, Haggai says it is because they have built their own houses but let go the house of God. This is the tragedy of misplaced values. God wills that we give and sacrifice to Him and His work so He might pour out a blessing to us beyond our ability to contain.

They thought little of Him. "Of the Rock that begat thee thou art unmindful." No doubt Moses was thinking of the time God had called him into conference to set down the Ten Commandments. That meeting was suddenly interrupted when God told Moses the people had betrayed Him by worshiping at a strange altar. Wending his way down the mountain, Moses sees the repulsive sight of twisting naked bodies writhing in pagan worship before an Egyptian calf-god. Repulsed, he slams the God-written stones into the mountain and goes to deal with a weak-willed people.

Too often we forget God when we are not near His house or His people. However, God desires our thoughts be continually on Him and His way. The Psalmist said,

"But his delight is in the law of the Lord; and in his law doth he meditate day and night" (Ps. 1:2). Here is the secret to a victorious Christian life. If God is the center of our thinking, then He will be the director of our emotions and the pilot of our lives. We then do not need the sight of the sanctuary or the presence of a preacher to keep us holy. If we learn to let Him be the center of our thoughts our lives will be holy and righteous.

Hunger of Heart

Not only does Moses make accusations but he also tells the tragic turn of events that follows such negligence, "They shall be burnt with hunger, and devoured with burning heat, and with bitter destruction." Not many years were to pass before Israel was staggered by such a hunger. Moses' prophecies were more than fulfilled in the heart-rending captivity they experienced.

One of the other great prophets looked to the time of one captivity and said sadly, "Behold the days come, saith the Lord God, that I will send a famine in the land, not a famine of bread, nor a thirst for water, but of hearing the words of the Lord" (Amos 8:11). Amos goes on to lament, "And they shall wander from sea to sea and from the north even to the east, they shall run to and fro to seek the words of the Lord, and shall not find it." This searching, searing, burning, feverish hunger for God's Word developed in Israel when they forgot and forsook God. For four hundred years God was silent and only broke that throbbing loneliness with the voice in the wilderness proclaiming the coming of Christ.

Ignoring the Lord

In our era of increased knowledge and scientific jargon there is a trend to replace the mourner's bench with the psychiatrist's couch. Often our sermons are designed to make people "feel" good rather than "be" good. Decay of spirit and religious death result when Christians forget the faithfulness the Spirit brings. This is what happened at Laodicea.

Established by Epaphras, the church of Laodicea was an immediate success. Situated in the heart of a great city, in just a few months the church had grown to a powerful force in community life. Laodicea was one of the most prosperous of Asian cities. From there came the most beautiful of glossy black wool and rich linen. A famous medical school was located in the city from which came an eye salve called collurium. The city was also a banking center.

However, in such an environment of prosperity the church faltered. Christ, in The Revelation, warns of lack of devotion, encouraging them to seek spiritual gold, raiments, and eye salve from God. He accuses them of spiritual pride, but at the same time extends His gracious invitation: "Behold, I stand at the door and knock: if any man hear my voice, and open the door, I will come in to him, and will sup with him, and he with me" (Rev. 3:20).

Often this Scripture is quoted to the unconverted, picturing the evangelistic Christ desiring entrance to the sinner's heart. However, it should be remembered these words were meant for a backslidden and unconcerned church. It is indeed sad to see the One who gave His life for the church, standing outside, desiring entrance.

Solomon further illustrates this tragic picture in the moving and majestic story of the captured mind asleep in the luxury of the king's palace. She is awakened by the insistent knocking of her Shepherd lover. From the cold night comes his voice, "Open to me, my sister, my love, my dove, my undefiled: for my head is filled with dew, and my locks with the drops of night" (Song of Sol. 5:2).

Sleepily, the bride answers. "I have put off my coat; how shall I put it on? I have washed my feet; how shall I defile them?" So thoroughly is she at ease and so sleepy that she does not wish to respond to the continual knocking. Finally, stricken by conscience, she goes to the door; but to her dismay her lover is gone. Frightened that he had left her, she hurries into the night, seeking him, only to be attacked. "The watchmen that went about the city found me, they wounded me; and the keepers of the walls took away my veil from me" (5:7).

In the light of this Scripture passage the scene of the knocking Christ becomes heartbreaking and frightening. The fact is, if the sleeping church does not arise, Christ can and will withdraw. The church, looking for the Lord who left, falls into great tribulation. Christ said, "So then because thou art lukewarm, and neither cold nor hot, I will spew thee out of my mouth" (Rev. 3:16).

How different the church at Ephesus! They too had received a stinging rebuke because they had left their first love. Christ warned them to remember, repent, and return. They did not ignore the warning but repented. History records results of both attitudes. The Laodicean church which neglected to heed advice was cast from the presence of God. Islamic invaders swept into the city and utterly destroyed it. The rich church of the Laodiceans lay in ruin and death came to slumbering saints.

Meanwhile, the Ephesian church prospered after their return to the altar. In fact so great was their revival that ten years after John the Beloved died the church was stronger than ever. The Emperor Trajan sent Pliny to that city to investigate whether the Christians should be persecuted. Pliny wrote back that Christianity had so flourished that the heathen temples were almost neglected and persecution would mean city-wide rebellion.

The fruit of the Spirit is faithfulness to our calling, and in this age of slumbering saints and dying sinners, this fruit needs cultivation more than any other.

9

The Shape of Contents

Famed painter Ben Shahn speaks with artistic clarity seldom equaled among his peers. Once he wished to portray fire so vividly none could misunderstand his meaning. This is not an easy task, since fire conjures up many images and feelings in our minds.

To one lost in the dark of a forest the sight of fire in camp brings overwhelming relief. When hunger strikes, fire can remind of sizzling steaks and crackling hams. Fire is also destructive and the horrors of a burning house with screaming children can be imagined. To others, whipped by chill winds of winter, fire is a friend gently lapping up logs in a lazy fireplace. However, Shahn wanted to picture fire in all its fury as a killer without mercy. To do this he painted a ravenous wolf with vicious fangs and fiery fur hungrily seeking a prey. One cannot view his masterpiece without getting the clear and shocking message Shahn wanted to communicate.

Words, like fire, often mean many different things to different people. Sometimes we need a clear and concise picture to give the shape of content in the author's words. The problem is further complicated by the fact that words are constantly changing their meaning. For example, at one time the word *girl* was defined as *a young person of either sex* while a *harlot* was simply a *fellow*. To be *lewd* once meant to just be *ignorant* and a *villain* was simply a *farm worker*. In Shakespeare's time *nice* was defined as *foolish* and *rheumatism* was a *head cold*. Because of these problems, sometimes we need to re-examine some preconceived ideas about things read and readjust our thinking accordingly. This is particularly true when we read, "The fruit of the Spirit is meekness."

A Vertical Meekness

When we hear the word *meekness*, immediately we think of a Walter Mitty character who has little in him that is desirable. Tragically, this is a gross misunderstanding of Paul's admonition, because meekness is not weakness, but strength. Perhaps a word picture can be drawn to give the shape of content so we might know what Paul means when he talks of meekness.

Michael Drury recently spoke of meekness by saying, "Humility so often seems vaguely desirable, but not really attractive. It might get one to heaven, but it won't promote a raise in pay. It sounds somewhat spineless, incompatible with intellect and a vigorous spirit." He went on to add that actually the reverse is true. The figures we commonly associate with humility—Jesus, Lincoln, Gandhi, Einstein—were not men of timid natures, but men who, while recognizing their weakness, also remembered their destinies and acted accordingly. He concluded by saying, "Humility is not self-disparagement; it is a tough, free, confident characteristic." This comes nearest to a real description of Paul's meaning.

What is often misunderstood concerning meekness is that to which this quality relates. Meekness is our attitude toward God, not man. It is vertical, not horizontal. This is why really meek men like those mentioned had such great and free spirits. If meekness related to man, then we would bend at a stronger person's will. In this case Christians could never take a place of leadership in communities or even live with any degree of dignity in a community. It must be clearly understood when Paul speaks of the fruit of the Spirit being meekness, this describes one's attitude toward God, not man. Then when our attitude toward God is one of meekness, our attitude toward man is one flavored with the same spirit. Meekness then becomes not a spineless wavering, but a force causing us to stand and do the will of God in the face of every foe. Meekness is not like Reuben: "unstable as water." Rather, it is like Joseph: "his bow abode in strength."

Moses Gives Meaning

To help paint a word picture perhaps it would be well to call on Moses, since the Bible says, "Now the man Moses was very meek, above all the men which were upon the face of the earth" (Num. 12:3). At least three incidents in his life point to this character trait and relate what deep and meaningful meekness is.

Response to his calling. After forty years in exile Moses is suddenly confronted with a miracle he does not understand. God speaks, telling Moses that he has been chosen to lead the Israelites out of Egypt. In response Moses asks honestly, "Who am I that I should go unto Pharaoh?" To this God responds, "I will be with you." Again, Moses asks, "Who shall I say sent me?" and God replies, "I am that I am." Moses continues to argue, saying they would not believe him and that he was slow of speech. God overrides these objections and Moses is commissioned to go.

The significance of all this lies in the contrast between his response and that of his actions forty years earlier. Then Moses had found an Egyptian beating one of his fellow countrymen, and he immediately rose up and killed the oppressor. Exile resulted and during those forty years God taught Moses very carefully that there are many battles that cannot be won with brawn. Spiritual battles are never won by hands of flesh. Paul sounds the clarion warning, "For we wrestle not against flesh and blood, but against principalities, against powers, against the rulers of the darkness of this world, against spiritual wickedness in high places. Wherefore take unto you the whole armor of God" (Eph. 6:12, 13a). Moses had learned by hard experience the futility and frustration of taking things into his own hands and trying to right wrongs with hands of flesh. Now, he simply stood before God and plainly admitted he was nothing. This is real meekness.

The songwriter has said so eloquently, "I am weakness, full of weakness, at Thy sacred feet I bow. Blest divine, eternal spirit, fill with power, and fill me now." Just as our spiritual life is predicated on the premise of remaining in the Vine, so our spiritual victories are only won as we humbly stand before God and admit our weakness and pray for His strength. Moses was completely honest in his approach to God, and this is real meekness.

His personal family problem. Moses had married a woman distrusted and hated by his sister and brother. The Bible says, "And Miriam and Aaron spake against Moses, because of the Ethiopian woman whom he married." Greater men with greater minds have pondered the reason for this disapproval. However, whether it was racial or personal on Miriam's part, is not important. The important thing is to note the reaction of Moses during this time of personal crisis and severe criticism. He did not react violently or spend time defending himself. Rather, he continued his work for God and let God work out the problem.

As time passed, the Lord suddenly spoke to all three individuals and called them before Himself. As they entered the tabernacle Miriam and Aaron are called forward and God sternly queries, "With him will I speak mouth to mouth . . . wherefore, then were ye not afraid to speak against my servant Moses?" Miriam is struck with leprosy and her punishment for the insurrection is known throughout the camp.

Note again, Moses then prays for his sister and after seven days she is healed. Again, we see no malice in the heart of Moses because he had been attacked in an area of life where most of us would have screamed with pain. Moses' attitude of meekness before God was such he did not need to defend himself or avenge himself.

Meekness is understanding perfectly our worth before God and knowing His forgiveness. Because Moses was meek before God and had settled his personal fears and frustrations, those of others could not spill over on him, causing him to react out of character with his calling. Embedded in this bit of sacred history is an important psychological fact. By perfectly understanding our status with the Savior, all the fear, frustrations, and inhibitions which plagued us before Calvary are erased. Here is the miracle of the new birth. Even though our environment might have contributed to all sorts of emotional problems and complexes, yet, in the new start and making peace with our Maker, we are emotionally sound and stable.

When we realize it is God who made us and not we ourselves, that we are the sheep of His pasture, that the steps of a good man are ordered by the Lord, then what does it matter what man might say. This is when real meekness toward God gives us strength in the face of our foes. Then we will not bow to the whims and wishes of those about us. We will not react to their frustration because we know we have been accepted by the Maker of the universe and our steps are ordered by Him. Therefore, criticism does not affect us and revenge is foreign to our characters.

His great disappointment. Moses had displeased God at Meribah and for this was not permitted to go into the Promised Land. This was one of the greatest blows Moses received. He had longed for the time he could lead the

105

people into their destined homeland. For forty years he had half-led, half-driven a nomadic nation toward home, but in old age, when sentiment is strong, he could not go in. Needless to say, his heart was crushed and his disappointment deep.

Yet, in all of this Moses did not strike out at God, but accepted his punishment like the great man he was. Like Job, he did not sin with his lips or charge God foolishly. Note the great qualities of meekness: absolute trust and reliance on the great wisdom and mercy of God. If God would not permit entrance, then Moses saw no need to whimper. Rather, he accepted God's ruling and went on from there. His faith was not shattered, but strengthened.

At a graveside a pastor will often say to a weeping widow, "God is too wise to ever make a mistake and too loving to ever be unkind." These are not just empty words or beautiful phrases to soothe an aching heart. These are truths throbbing through history and if we could grasp fully their meaning we would catch some of the spirit of Moses. Rather than rebel when we do not see eye to eye with God as to how His business should be run, what a thrill it would be if we in the meekness of Moses can be content with a Mount Pisgah experience. This is real meekness. Indeed as the psalmist sang, "His way is perfect."

Beneath the Veneer

Since it is certain that meekness concerns man's relationship to God rather than to his fellow man, perhaps it would be wise to reexamine those times we come before His throne in worship. God has promised, "The meek also shall increase their joy in the Lord . . ." (Isa. 29:19). This is true because the man who is really meek before God comes with absolute honesty and helplessness before the throne of God. And in this freedom of honesty there is great and wonderful joy.

Sadly, some of us have built a system of worship that is not conducive to meekness before God. If we can break down this veneer of pharisaical worship, be brutally honest about ourselves to God, our worship becomes richer and more meaningful. Tragically, much worship is self-centered and reflects little of the meekness which is the fruit of the Spirit. If we could remember that true worship is God-centered, rather than self-centered, then meekness becomes a part of us.

A young girl, very excited because her boyfriend had finally come to church, rose to testify. She was thrilled because God had faithfully answered her prayers and nervous because she wanted her testimony to make just the right impression. She blurted out, "I'm so glad that I'm so wonderful."

We laugh when we read about an incident such as this, which must have been a real embarrassment to the young lady. She had meant to say, "I'm so glad that He is so wonderful."

However, this incident reveals that very often worship can center around self rather than God. Paul warned young Timothy; "This know also, that in the last days perilous times shall come. For men shall be lovers of their own selves . . . more than lovers of God" (2 Tim. 3:1-4).

In The Revelation an angel gives us the true key to worship. John had been exiled on the Isle of Patmos and while there God revealed His plan for ages to come. In one case the revelation came through a "mighty angel." Afterward, John fell to worship the heavenly being. He records, "And I fell at his feet to worship him. And he said unto me, See thou do it not: I am thy fellowservant, and of thy brethren that have the testimony of Jesus: worship God . . ." (Rev. 19:10).

Here is the key found throughout the Word of God by prophets, priests, and angels: "Worship God only!" Jesus said, "Thou shalt worship the Lord thy God, and him only shalt thou serve" (Matt. 4:10).

107

Men today would argue that our worship does center only around God. Perhaps this is completely true in many lives. However, it would be well to evaluate our worship and see if it is God-centered or self-centered.

The songs we sing. A very interesting experiment is leafing through the pages of a hymnal and noting all of the songs with personal pronouns in the titles. A deeper study of these songs often reveals the majority of them center around us and our feelings rather than God. Notice the titles: "I Love to Tell the Story," "I'm Glad I'm One of Them," "I Would Not Be Denied," "I Shall Not Be Moved," "Follow, I will Follow Thee," and "I Surrender All." One noted minister observed in the favorite song, "In the Garden," there are twenty-seven references to oneself while only a few to God.

These, of course, are songs of testimony and are very useful in some of our worship. The point is that perhaps we should include in our worship more hymns that have references to God, His greatness, His love, His concern for man. The emphasis in our worship is not on our righteousness, but His. Like Moses we ask, Who are we? There are great worship songs like: "All Hail the Power of Jesus' Name," "Great Is Thy Faithfulness," "Praise Him! Praise Him," "He Is Able to Deliver Thee," and "Jesus Paid It All." Could there be a greater song to emphasize God's greatness than:

> To God be the glory, great things He hath done,
> So loved He the world that He gave us His Son,
> Who yielded His life an atonement for sin,
> And opened the Life Gate that all may go in.
> Praise the Lord, praise the Lord, let the earth hear his voice;
> Praise the Lord, praise the Lord, let the people rejoice;
> Oh, come to the Father, thro' Jesus the Son,
> And give Him the glory; great things He has done.

The congregation had just finished singing, "Still Sweeter Every Day," when an elderly man stood and very innocently said, "You know, folks, I'm just like that song. I'm getting sweeter every day."

Most of us have heard testimonies like this and they bring a smile to our lips. Since witnessing is part of our worship, there are some guidelines to be followed in testifying for our Master.

Recently a very sincere man stood and went into great detail about how many souls he had won to Christ. Of course, the testimony was not as effective as it could have been because the emphasis was on himself rather than on how Christ worked through him. Sometimes we unconsciously give ourselves credit for God's work.

Testimonies are very effective for bringing souls to Christ. They are not showcases for our own spirituality or religious wisdom. When they are, the effectiveness is gone. Christ, speaking of the manner in which He would die, said "And I, if I be lifted up from the earth, will draw all men unto me" (John 12:32). Perhaps this Scripture should be remembered when we testify. He is to be exalted. Our testimonies will be soul-stirring and soul-winning if we confess with the hymnwriter: "Lord, now indeed I find thy power, and thine alone, can change the leper's spots and melt the heart of stone."

Jesus condemned the Pharisee who called attention to his own worth and to the sinner's evil. He admonished us to pray not to impress men, but to commune with God. Therefore, our prayers should always be a practice in honesty toward God—honesty of our own inabilities and His strength.

A good question to ask oneself is, "Are my prayers completely selfish?" Try listening to yourself pray. Are your prayers always for your needs, your family's needs? Or, do your prayers encompass the needs of others? Can the Holy Spirit move you to pray for others, forgetting self?

Jesus gave the perfect pattern for prayer when His disciples asked Him to teach them to pray. The prayer He taught is two-thirds praise, with the basic message centering around God's will rather than self-centered interests. The emphasis is always on God. Prayer can be a great adventure if we can break through our own self-ishness and follow freely His Spirit as He takes us to many places in prayer. Selfish prayers yield small harvests, but God-directed, self-less prayers bring an abundance of fruit.

While it is necessary to "take heed unto thyself," yet we should press on beyond this point in prayer into the wider plains of complete abandonment of self in praise and prayer. May this be our experience when we pray:

And when, before the throne, I stand in Him complete,
Jesus died my soul to save, my lips shall still repeat.

Some sing robustly, "The Love of God," especially that last beautiful verse. Do we really believe it? So often we measure His love by our own fickle, changing love. We compare it to the purest love we know, that of a mother or father for the child. Yet, it is far more than this. Fathers can be cruel and mothers without love. Not God! When we confine His love to our own, are we not saying in effect, "I love as much as God." Is this self-worship?

Many are frustrated and will continue to be so as long as they limit God's love and understanding to human standards. Can we not understand He loves us far more than we love ourselves? He loves our loved ones far more than we do. Why should we fear? Why should we be uncertain? Why should we live below our privileges as Christians?

David said, "Whither shall I go from thy spirit? or whither shall I flee from thy presence? If I ascend up into heaven, thou art there: if I make my bed in hell, behold thou art there. If I take the wings of the morning, and dwell in the uttermost parts of the sea; Even there shall thy hand lead me, and thy right hand shall follow me" (Ps. 139:10). If we could just accept this love we would really know that love that passes understanding and have a tranquillity that only such love can bring.

Satan often defeats Christians because they do not understand God's mercy and love and they feel unworthy of that love which they do understand. Therefore, when they pray they are always asking to be made worthy. We could never be worthy. We do not ask for justice, just mercy. God did not love us because we were worthy. In fact, we will never understand why He chose to love us. All we can say is:

> Upon that cross of Jesus mine eyes at times can see
> The very dying form of One who suffered there for me;
> And from my smitten heart with tears, two wonders I confess,
> The wonders of His glorious love and my own worthlessness.

So often people say to their pastor, "I don't feel like praising God this morning. That's why I did not respond when you called for worship." Is this not worshiping our feelings rather than our God? Worship is not based on feeling, but on the fact that God desires the praises of His people. There is a "sacrifice of praise." It should be remembered God inhabits the praises of His own.

Paul mentions the trying battle between the flesh and spirit. An eternal battle it is; it is fought within each of us. Fatigue, illness, or emotional strains can make it hard to worship. However, we should remember to worship Him at all times, regardless of feelings. When we succumb to the temptations to let down in our worship because of feelings at that moment, our worship is self-centered rather than God-directed. Perhaps we should shake ourselves and make this grim determination:

> No longer will I stay within the valley,
> I'll climb to mountain heights above;
> The world is dying now for want of someone
> To tell them of the Savior's matchless love.

Jesus Paid It All

May our prayer always be that our worship will always be God-centered. We worship not to impress or to be

111

impressed. We worship because Jesus paid it all. If our worship has been self-centered perhaps we should drop our head and on our knees before him pray:

> For nothing good have I whereby thy grace to claim—
> I'll wash my garments white in the blood of Calvary's Lamb.
> Jesus paid it all, all to Him I owe;
> Sin had left a crimson stain, He washed it white as snow.

When we worship in absolute meekness and have evidence of this fruit in our lives, our bearing becomes pleasing to God and witnesses to men. Plutarch once asked how the fig tree, whose branches, stems, roots, and leaves are so bitter, could bear such sweet and pleasant fruit. It may also be asked how the sweet fruits of the Spirit grow on the bitter stock of human nature. We may not know the answer, but we do know the result as we honestly and without pretense come before God in the meekness of Moses. Then we really learn to live.

10

Prisoner by Choice

A record 63-year prison term ended by death for 91-year-old Martin Dalton, formerly of Fall River, Massachusetts. Strangest was the fact that the last thirty years of prison were self-imposed. He had repeatedly turned down parole, saying, "The world has changed too much."

After serving thirty-three years for slaying a New York businessman in Rhode Island, Dalton was offered release and taken from his cell to view the outside world. He was astonished at the cars that clogged the streets, the new buildings, the changed fashions. When he had entered the prison before the turn of the century, horses still drew carriages along main street, bustles were in vogue, and life moved at a slower pace.

So, with family gone, no home, money, job, or friends, Dalton elected to stay in prison. He worked on the prison farm just outside the walls until his death. That was as far away as he wanted to go. He was a prisoner by choice.

Another man many years ago made the same decision, but under different circumstances. The apostle Paul wrote he was a prisoner of Jesus Christ by his own choosing. Many times he said he was a love slave of Christ.

Some have asked why Paul chose to suffer for Christ and be a prisoner by choice. Perhaps the question can best be answered by saying Paul had learned the secret of life. He came to know what so many great philosophers tried to learn and some did after years of study; there is freedom only in bondage. While the statement seems contradictory, still it is eternally true. The free and happy man is he who is a prisoner of moral laws and codes set down by the Creator. And, Paul says, "The fruit of the Spirit is temperance."

Out the "In" Door

Philosophers have pondered for ages why so many things seem pleasurable, but are forbidden by God and society. Omar Khayyam articulates the query of many,

> What! out of senseless nothing
> Create a conscious something, to resent the yoke
> Of unpermitted pleasures,
> And be under everlasting punishment if broke?

Khayyam frankly admits his quandary and his only solution is to eat, drink, and be merry. He feels the question cannot be answered and flatly states:

> Myself when young did eagerly frequent
> Doctor and Saint, and heard great argument
> About it and about; but evermore
> Came out the same door where in I went.

Yet, the testimony of those who have sought freedom through excesses, failing to acknowledge real freedom is only in bondage, reveals the tragedies of their philosophy. Lord Byron said on his last birthday, "The flowers and fruits of life are gone, the worm, the canker, and the grief are mine alone." He died at thirty-six, defeated and depressed.

114

There is an answer much better than merely resigning ourselves to the fate that awaits or coming out of the "in" door. The Bible is a compendium for behavior and it gives cogent reasons for following the admonitions of God. The reason why there are many temptations with resulting frustration if we follow them unchecked, is that God has created man with the potential for either great good or great evil. We are not machines programmed for certain responses, but rather free wills choosing the good or the evil, sharing in the consequences of that decision.

Greatness is never just strength. Hitler had strength to frighten a world and practically exterminate a race. Yet, no one would dare call him great. Nero's authority and strength remained unchallenged, but tarring Christians, lighting their still breathing bodies so his gardens might have night torches, is certainly not a display of greatness. Greatness is not just the display of strength, but also the restraint of strength. Lincoln was great because while he had the might to crush the South, he preached and practiced, "malice toward none, and charity for all." Washington could have been a dictator, but chose to restrain himself, desiring a strong democracy. Similarly, happiness is not free pursuit of our fancies, but also willful restraint of them.

Our lives are as rivers, either useful in their energies or destructive in their force. One can view the majesty of a plummeting waterfall channeled to bring electricity to a dark community or irrigation to a parched land and feel a sense of appreciation. Or, one can see a swirling undisciplined stream gushing out of its banks, eating away valuable farm land and creating havoc which years of labor cannot right, and feel frustration. The usefulness or destruction is not just in the water itself, but in how it is channeled. Similarly useful and meaningful lives can come only from the temperate hearts which have passions, channeled for the greatest good. We are bundles of passions, desires, emotions, and feelings, and inherent in them all is great good or great evil. Paul says the Spirit-filled life is one that is channeled and disciplined for greatest good.

The Heart of the Soul

However, temperance is not just the outward sign of a well-disciplined life. Temperance, as the fruit of the Spirit, goes to the heart of the soul and is the very character of man. Thousands of thieves are locked behind bars and sealed off from society. However, they still are thieves who simply do not have opportunity to commit their crimes against a free society. This is true of other crimes and offenses. The miracle of Christ is that man's character is changed and not just his environment. Men who find Christ are not just locked up, but cleaned up and given a new start where all old things are passed away. Temperance, then, is the very motive of the soul.

David, who learned discipline from bitter experience, prayed, "Let the words of my mouth, and the meditations of my heart be acceptable in thy sight, O Lord, my strength and my redeemer" (Ps. 19:14). This is real temperance. There is the outward discipline, the watch over the words of his mouth, but also discipline of heart and soul. David pleads that his very thoughts and motives will be pleasing to God.

When persons are so motivated they remain true regardless of circumstances or environment. There is no lost weekend or time when, away from the sight of the sanctuary, they let go and live as they really want. David's sin came when he failed to pray and live that prayer. The real prisoner who knows great freedom is not in bondage to society, mate, family, or friends, but rather a love slave to God.

Allegiance to Christ through the Holy Spirit brings out our best while the undisciplined obedience to our lower nature destroys like a flash-flood, eroding emotional stability and physical well-being of ourselves and those about us. Paul says the man filled with the Spirit will have self-control.

Getting Control

A young mother was having trouble with a five-year-old whining and showing off. After soundly disciplining him and sending him off to bed she explained, "Maybe I'm old fashioned, but I can't believe that being allowed to make everybody else miserable now will make him more lovable twenty years from now." Her idea was that discipline is more than punishment or reward. Discipline is actually putting children in control of themselves so they can use their best qualities. It is the question of giving them ability to make decisions and to accept the consequences of their choice.

While temperance is a most desirable fruit of the Spirit, the honest man will wonder how to bring it into play in his own life. This is where the Bible gives some very practical help, showing how we can gain control of ourselves. Just as the mother with the unruly child, we can be put in charge of ourselves by practical pointers from God's Word. Strangely, these coincide with advice given by leading psychologists relative to the same problems.

Strong self-discipline. Jesus talked of four kinds of soil in which the good seed fell. Only one soil was "disciplined" and produced fruit. By this parable He says much depends on us in this matter of living the overcoming life. Paul would add later, "Every man that striveth for mastery is temperate in all things. Now they do it to obtain a corruptible crown. . . . but we an incorruptible. But I keep under my body, and bring it into subjection: lest that by any means, when I have preached to others, I myself should be a castaway" (1 Cor. 9:25, 26).

At the end of his great life, Paul would take time in that dismal prison to give his last will and testament to a young preacher in Ephesus. In 2 Timothy 2:4 Paul

117

provides his son in the faith three important rules for self-discipline. The first is, "No man that warreth entangleth himself with the affairs of this life; that he may please him who hath chosen him to be a soldier." In other words, living for Christ is a full-time job. This did not mean Timothy was to isolate himself from all associations or employment in his community. Paul himself while preaching also worked as a tentmaker to supply his physical needs. The crux of the question is that one who has been listed for Christ's service should keep his eye on the ultimate goal. There are no vacations from God or His work.

Dr. Smiley Blanton, prominent psychiatrist, says, "In nine cases out of ten, where temptation is concerned, the ultimate disadvantages far outweigh the momentary satisfaction." He went on to show that drinks are never worth the hangover or the illicit sexual encounter the ulimate consequence. Paul was telling Timothy the same thing. Timothy is admonished to remember his destiny when youthful lust or temptations come and to foresee the consequences so he will be an overcomer. He must not become entangled with the world.

Next, Paul says there are certain rules which must be observed, "And if a man also strives for masteries, yet is he not crowned, except he strives lawfully" (v. 5). Some feel they get away with their sins. Yet, this is never the case. While the voice of conscience may be a whisper, still the penalty for ignoring it is great, as any psychiatrist or doctor can tell you. Dr. Blanton also said, "Whether you consider conscience a divinely implanted mechanism, a dim echo of parental authority, or the ancient and collective taboos of the human race, it remains the device in human peronality that triggers one of the most destructive of all emotions: guilt."

We really never escape ourselves and the voice that speaks to us in the stillness of our souls. Men may never find out about our sins, but we are constantly pricked by their sharp and hurting edges. And, as Paul said, we can never really stand tall, look men straight in the eyes, master any situation until we keep the rules laid down. It is relatively unimportant if we are caught or not caught. Religion goes beneath the veneer of human pretension and is the stuff of the soul. We only fool ourselves when we think we can get away with striving unlawfully.

The final thought Paul gives is "The husbandmen that laboreth must be first partaker of the fruits" (v. 6). Some people talk about religion to cover some terrible deficiencies in their own lives. The incident of the woman at the well is a case in point. When Christ came too close to her problem she tried to steer Him off with a religious question as to the proper place to worship. Jesus briefly answers and then gets to the heart of the real issue.

Religion can become a shield for the self-righteous and we well deserve some of the criticism the world gives us. Paul recognizes this in many passages, but particularly here he talks to Timothy about being a partaker of what he is preaching. Timothy might argue religion or theological questions all his life and still be lost. Not every man that says "Lord, Lord" will enter in. The important thing, Paul says, is that we partake of the mercy, and the discipline of Christ. Then we are masters of our lives. We are in control of ourselves at the moment we live in the attitude of which Paul speaks. So, the first step toward self-control is a will to live by the rules, and discipline ourselves to His laws.

Know yourself. While philosophers have said this through the ages we sometimes fail to feel the force of its truth. This was the heart of Socrates' sermons and much of what the New Testament is all about. Peter says, "And beside this, add to your faith virtue, and to your virtue knowledge. And to knowledge temperance" (2 Peter 1:5). Peter says to add to our virtue knowledge, or in other words, know our limitations and His strength.

Different temptations appeal to different people, with varying degrees of intensity. What might be a stumbling block to you might not be to your neighbor. This is one of the reasons Christ taught us not to judge another's actions or reactions. We cannot appreciate their dilemma because we do not know the problems that plague them. However, if we chart our own weaknesses and practice a little self-honesty as to the flaws in our character, then much of our problem is eliminated. It is true, temptations usually do not lie in wait for us, but actually there are flaws in our characters which impel us to seek out the temptations. For example, the philanderer will always have a succession of romantic advances made to him because he subconsciously creates those situations.

There is only one way to conquer when we have been tempted or we have sought out temptation. That is to obey the Bible's admonition to flee from it. Too often most of us just crawl away hoping it will overcome us. The secret to success in living a temperate life is to chart our weaknesses, avoid contacts in areas in which we are vulnerable and then if we are in the situation, flee. Joseph found this his salvation with Potiphar's wife. If you are extremely ambitious, then one must flee the temptation of cutting corners and throats to get to the top. If you are acutely dissatisfied with your state in life you must avoid, like the plague, the temptation to escapism through drink, pills, or fantasies. Knowing yourself is the wisdom Peter suggests in times of temptation.

Put on Christ. Paul writes, "But put on the Lord Jesus Christ, and make not provisions for the flesh" (Rom. 13:14). It may sound trite to simply say, "Pray about it," but it still works. One psychiatrist explained it like this: "After a long life spent observing human behavior, I have no doubt whatever, that entirely apart from its religious significance, prayer is one of the most effective methods of tapping the wisdom and power that exist in the great reservoir of the unconscious."

He went on to add that lest he be misunderstood he did not think a mere repetition or recitation of a prayer would be sufficient. He said, "In effective prayer there must be humility, relinquishment of desires, acknowledgment of helplessness. The psychiatrist cannot explain this fully, anymore than the theologian can, but he knows that it is so. Self-surrender is the key. When this attitude pervades the conscious mind and sinks deeply into the unconscious, the result is serenity and clarity of thought that make right decisions not only possible, but almost inevitable." Freud also observed, "Intelligence can function reliably only when removed from the influence of strong emotional force." While some people may disagree with the application of this principle, it is still true that prayer draws us away from the strong emotional pull of that temptation and puts us in touch with the source of all intelligence. Therefore, wisdom comes into our hearts. James simply says, "If any of you lack wisdom, let him ask of God, that giveth to all men liberally" (1:5).

Great prayers in the past illustrate the power of this force. The Bible quickly admits that outstanding prophets had the same desires, passions, and drives we have. However, through the power of prayer they were able to channel these drives to God's ultimate purpose. The world is much better for their doing so. Prayer works and is virtually an untapped resource for strong and confident living.

Be filled with the Spirit. Paul gives us one of those sobering truths with such utter simplicity it staggers us. He simply says, "And be not drunk with wine, wherein is excess; but be filled with the Spirit" (Eph. 5:18). As intoxicating wine has sway over a body so the Spirit has sway as we are filled with it. Paul believed and preached that when one is so absorbed with the Spirit he is overpowered by a force greater than himself. In other words there is a higher plane of living as one is charged through the continual presence of God through His indwelling Spirit. It then becomes more than self-control, it is Christ-control. As we all have found out, this is the only way to rise above our own natures.

121

Up from the Pit

Much of our happiness or unhappiness depends on our ability to handle temptation—instead of letting it handle us. Robert Louis Stevenson said, "We are condemned to some nobility," while the Bible says, "The wages of sin is death." God has created us with the ability and desire for greatness and nobility. If we stifle that drive our lives become shattered and dissipated. If we cultivate that nobility we move from the realm of animalism closer to divinity.

Jesus once told a story of a boy who drank of both natures. The Prodigal Son had gone from the peak to the pit and finally back to the peak. One weeps as he reads of the great forgiveness of the father and the deep shame of the son. Through it all there beats a certain sadness as we think of the young life so wasted and useless. Then, Christ turns to talk of the elder brother and his wrong reaction. After rebuke for his attitude the father speaks words that ring with clarity through the ages. Perhaps like them, we have felt we can never really appreciate the forgiveness of Christ until we taste, like the Prodigal Son, the husks for hogs, or maybe we feel we are unappreciated for our goodness. In either case the words of the kindly and kingly father are warm and wonderful.

"Son," he says to the older boy, "You are ever with me, and all that I have is yours." The father knew that although he had forgiven the Prodigal, the son could never forgive himself. There would always be periods of deep regret because he had disappointed his father and all those of the household. The father reminds the oldest son, "You are ever with me." In other words, he would never have moments of remorse and could always hold his head up unashamed. A feast was necessary to show the younger was forgiven, but not so with the older. The father simply said, "All that I have is yours."

It is not necessarily true that the most wayward is the most thankful. Therefore, by refusing to live the undisciplined life we save ourselves from many scars and heartbreaks. The harvest of sins still comes long after Christ forgives, and this is why it is so important to learn the life of temperance and remain true to Christ from youth. Paul said the fruit of the Spirit is temperance.

If ever we lived in an age when temperance is needed it is now. Our society has sown the wind and is reaping the whirlwind. A Senate survey recently showed some two-and-one-half million children from ages ten to seventeen have a police record. Add to this the knowledge that 85 percent of all our criminals are under twenty-five years of age. For our society there is an answer. As we live a temperate life and inspire our children to do so, our world can change. Excess demands greater excess and only the discipline of the spirit can break the circle of selfishness. The writer of Ecclesiastes had tasted all the excesses of life and yet in his final moment he only pleads, "Remember now thy Creator in the days of thy youth, while the evil days come not, nor the years draw nigh, when thou shalt say, I have no pleasure in them" (12:1).

Shakespeare said, "There is a tide in the affairs of men, which taken at the flood, leads on to fortune: omitted, all the voyage of their life is bound in shallows and in miseries: And we must take the current when it serves, or lose our venture." What is true of individuals is also true of nations. We have been staggered by the riots that rip our cities and violence that shatters our homes. The tide for temperance has now risen and for our own survival we must take it. The fruit of the Spirit is temperance.

Temperance seems to be the last, the crowning fruit of the Spirit. Live in the spirit of these great lines!

> Self-reverence, self-knowledge, self-control,
> These three alone lead life to sovereign power;
> Yet not for power (power by herself
> Would come uncalled for) but to live by law
> Acting the law we live by without fear
> And because right is right, to follow right
> Were wisdom, in the scorn of consequence.

123

11

Fortune in a Bottle

Fifty-five-year-old Jack Wurm had reached the depths of despair and depression. He was on the beach both literally and figuratively a few years ago, broken and discouraged. He had failed in business and now was killing time walking along the California beach between job interviews.

As he plowed through the sand his eyes fell on a half-hidden bottle and it appeared something was in it. He kicked it idly and then stooped to examine the bottle. A note was inside, so he broke it open and read, "To avoid confusion I leave my entire estate to the lucky person who finds this bottle and to my attorney, Barry Cohen, share and share alike. Daisy Alexander. June 20, 1937."

The name Daisy Alexander did not mean anything to Jack Wurm so he passed it off as some sort of joke. However, later he learned Daisy Alexander was heiress to the vast Singer Sewing Machine fortune and if he could prove the validity of the note he would be entitled to half of her 12-million-dollar fortune.

Research revealed Daisy Singer Alexander was an eccentric who lived in England. She often tossed bottles into the water wondering where they went. She died at age eighty-one in 1939, leaving no final will. Wurm claimed the fortune and the case began to wend its way through the complicated court procedures. An ocean-current expert testified that a bottle dropped in the Thames River could wash to the English Channel, then to the North Sea, through the Bering Straits, into the North Pacific and end up in either California or Mexico. He said the journey would take approximately twelve years. It actually took eleven years and nine months. Jack Wurm had found a fortune in a bottle.

Shuffling through the Scripture looking for a sense of direction we have stumbled onto a spiritual fortune in a bottle. The fruit of the Spirit in all nine poignant portraits unlocks for us the riches of the Christ-centered personality. The thrill of the find is great and the fortune eternal. Now that we have taken and examined each individually, perhaps it would be wise to again look at the whole in context.

Paul pits these spiritual qualities against the pulls of the flesh. He warns that the fruit of the flesh is sexual immorality, impurity of mind, sensuality, idolatry, witchcraft, hatred, quarreling, jealousy, bad temper, rivalry, factions, a party spirit, envy, drunkenness, and orgies. Paul then lists the personality of the true believer. It is necessary to mention again that these fruits are not separate traits from which we can choose those most appealing to us; all are a unit; each complements the others. The fruit of the flesh brings death and destruction while the fruit of the Spirit brings life and peace.

As in any contrast there is a decision. Joshua challenged Israel to choose this day who to serve; the daily choice of good or evil is ours. The Psalmist prayed, ". . . unite my heart to fear thy name" (86:11), and this prayer must be ours if the fruit of the Spirit is to be cultivated.

Paul, in another of his profound statements says, "Ye are God's husbandry. . . . Ye are God's building . . ." (1 Cor. 3:9). With our Western minds it is sometimes difficult to get the full implication of Paul's statement. J. B.

Phillips has suggested the following translation, ". . . you are a field under God's cultivation, or, if you like, a house being built to his plan." What a thought this is! We are fields being cultivated by God for beautiful fruits and productive plants. As any field must be plowed, seeded, weeded, and irrigated, so must God cultivate our lives.

The attitude of Paul was that although we are being driven toward perfection and indeed are being cultivated, still there is much to be done in our characters. He said, "Not as though I had already attained, either were already perfect. . . . But I follow after that I may apprehend that for which also I am apprehended of Christ Jesus" (Phil. 3:12). Then, admitting his imperfection he says, "Brethren, I count not myself to have apprehended" (v. 13a). But, he moves to the positive and the living hope, "But this one thing I do, forgetting those things which are behind, and reaching forth unto those things which are before" (v. 13b). Henry Wadsworth Longfellow expressed the thought another way:

> Let us then be up and doing
> With a heart for any fate.
> Still achieving, still pursuing,
> Learn to labor and to wait.

Paul also said we are buildings being constructed to God's specifications. God takes the timber of our lives and makes of us that which He desires we be. The important thing in both metaphors is that the work is now going on. In other words, just as fruit grows until it ripens, so we are cultivated and built by God until that time of perfection.

Here we have our fortune in a bottle. The fruit of the Spirit can and does grow in us until we are perfected in His sight. Once a man asked Rembrandt at what point a picture was complete. To this the famed Dutch artist replied, "A painting is finished when it expresses the intent of the artist." So it is with our lives. Our lives will be complete only when we express the full intent of the Master. This is what the fruit of the Spirit is all about. These qualities that were so in evidence in Christ's earthly life are qualities that express the intent of the Master Artist. Therefore, we actively seek His cultivation, His building, His pruning, until our lives are comformable to the image of His only Son.

Woodrow Wilson said, "Christianity has liberated the world, not as a philosophy of altruism but by its revelation of the power of unselfish love." This about sums up the purpose and content of the fruit of the Spirit. Much of the world still seeks to be liberated and the Great Commission will not be carried out by self-styled evangelism or high-powered programming but by the Spirit-filled and thrilled life, rich in the fruits of the Spirit, and overflowing with the full measure of God's love. Only then can we feel the heart throb of the suffering world and feel for the pain of a groaning creation. Zechariah says succinctly, "Not by might, nor by power, but by my spirit saith the Lord of hosts" (Zech. 4:6).

The fruit of the Spirit is love, joy, peace, longsuffering, gentleness, goodness, faith, meekness, and temperance. Christ so perfectly lived these, and as we think of that perfect Life and what He desires us to be, we say with the poet:

> The face of all the world has changed for me
> Since first I heard the footsteps of thy soul.